MODERNIST LITERATURE:
A GUIDE FOR THE PERPLEXED

The Guides For The Perplexed Series

Related titles include:

MODERNIST LITERATURE: A GUIDE FOR THE PERPLEXED

PETER CHILDS

continuum

Continuum International Publishing Group

The Tower Building	80 Maiden Lane
11 York Road	Suite 704
London SE1 7NX	New York, NY 10038

www.continuumbooks.com

British Library Cataloguing-in-Publication Data
A catalogue record for this book is available from the British Library.

ISBN: 978-0-8264-25980 (hardback)
978-0-8264-32629 (paperback)

Library of Congress Cataloging-in-Publication Data
A catalog record of this book is available from the Library of Congress.

Typeset by Newgen Imaging Systems Pvt Ltd, Chennai, India
Printed and bound in India

CONTENTS

TIMELINE
(COMPILED BY CLAIRE SMITH)

Year	Select Literary Works	Cultural Events	Historical and Scientific Notes
1890	Marie Corelli – *Wormwood*	Publication of William James's *The Principles of Psychology*, in which 'stream of consciousness' was coined.	British Empire spans a fifth of the world with 400 million people
	Henrik Ibsen – *Hedda Gabler*	William Morris' Kelmscott Press founded. Publishes limited luxury editions	Elementary education to be free in England
	Henry James – *The Tragic Muse*	Vincent Van Gogh – 'The Church at Auvers' Vincent Van Gogh dies (–1915) Publication of Sir James Frazer's work of anthropology *The Golden Bough: A Study in Magic and Religion* (12 volumes)	
1891	Thomas Hardy – *Tess of the D'Urbervilles*	Claude Monet – 'Haystacks'	McCormick Harvester (agriculture) producing 75,000 machines at its Chicago plant
	Oscar Wilde – *The Picture of Dorian Gray; Lord Arthur Savile's Crime and Other Stories*	Arthur Rimbaud dies	(–1892) International Peace Bureau founded and based in Berne, Switzerland
	Ménie Muriel Dowie – *A Girl in the Karpathians* (travelogue)		Pope Leo XIII's encyclical *Rerum novarum* counters socialism

Continued

Year	Select Literary Works	Cultural Events	Historical and Scientific Notes
	Walt Whitman – *Good-Bye My Fancy* and *Sands at Seventy* published in 'death bed' edition of *Leaves of Grass* George Gissing – *New Grub Street* William Morris – *The Story of the Glittering Plain; Poems by the Way; News from Nowhere* (first serialized in *Commonweal 1890*)		Electric generators come into use in copper industry in the United States
1892	Henrik Ibsen – *The Master Builder* Marie Corelli – *The Soul of Lilith* Charlotte Perkins Gilman – 'The Yellow Wall-paper' (published in *New England Magazine*) Arthur Conan Doyle – *The Adventures of Sherlock Holmes*	American poet Walt Whitman dies George Meredith elected president of The Society of Authors Exhibition of the work of Edvard Munch in Berlin (influence upon expressionism) (–1894) Claude Monet – 'Rouen Cathedral' Publication of Christina Rossetti's religious work *The Face of the Deep* Poet Alfred Tennyson dies	Invention of diesel engine by Rudolph Diesel Publication of Karl Pearson's *The Grammar of Science* William Gladstone becomes British prime minister (Liberal)
1893	George Gissing – *The Odd Women* Oscar Wilde – *A Woman of No Importance* Marie Corelli – *Barabbas* Christina Rossetti – *Verses*	Pierre-Auguste Renoir – 'Bather Arranging Her Hair' Publication of W. B. Yeats's essay collection *The Celtic Twilight*	Franco-Russian Alliance signed Grover Cleveland becomes U.S. president (Democrat) Model-T motor car invented by Henry Ford Wilhelm Maybach invents modern carburetor

Year	Select Literary Works	Cultural Events	Historical and Scientific Notes
1894	W. B. Yeats – *The Land of Heart's Desire* (play)	Publication of A. C. Swinburne's *Studies in Prose and Poetry*	Gramophone invented
	William Morris – *The Wood Beyond the World*		Earl of Rosebery becomes British prime minister (Liberal)
	A. C. Swinburne – *Astrophel and Other Poems*		Urban and Rural District Councils established in the United Kingdom
	(–1895) Rudyard Kipling – *The Jungle Books*		Death duties introduced in the United Kingdom
1895	H. G. Wells – *The Time Machine*	Max Nordau's *Degeneration* (1892) translated into English	X-Ray machine invented by William Röntgen
	Joseph Conrad – *Almayer's Folly*	Russian theorist Mikhail Bakhtin is born	Marquess of Salisbury becomes British prime minister (Conservative)
	Oscar Wilde – *The Importance of Being Earnest*	28 December –The Lumière Brothers' Cinématographe used for first time at Grand Café, Paris, signalling first motion picture.	Oscar Wilde is imprisoned.
	Marie Corelli – *The Sorrows of Satan*	Gustav Klimt – 'Love'	
	Ménie Muriel Dowie – *Gallia*	Exhibition of Paul Cézanne's work in Paris	
	George Meredith – *The Amazing Marriage*	Publication of Sigmund Freud's first work of psychoanalysis *Studies on Hysteria*	
	Thomas Hardy – *Jude the Obscure*	The Henry Wood Promenade Concerts begin at Queen's Hall	
	William Morris – *The Water of the Wondrous Isles*		
1896	Joseph Conrad – *An Outcast of the Islands*	First modern Olympic Games is held in Athens	Case of *Plessy* vs. *Ferguson*: Judge finds segregation on railway carriages in Louisiana to be inconsistent with American Constitution

Continued

Year	Select Literary Works	Cultural Events	Historical and Scientific Notes
	Edwin Arlington Robinson – *The Torrent and the Night Before*	William Morris dies	Wireless telegraph patented by Marconi.
	Anton Chekhov – *The Seagull*	Paul Verlaine dies	Radioactivity in uranium discovered by Antoine Becquerel.
	Christina Rossetti – *New Poems* (published posthumously)		Local councils begin construction of Council Houses.
	Marie Corelli – *The Murder of Delicia*; *The Mighty Atom*		Red Flag Act repealed – speed limits increased to 22 km.p.h. in United Kingdom.
	William Morris – *The Well at the World's End*		
1897	Henry James – *What Maisie Knew*; *The Spoils of Poynton*	Publication of Hugh Stutfield's article 'The Psychology of Feminism' in *Blackwood's Magazine*	World Zionist Organization founded
	Edwin Arlington Robinson – *The Children of the Night*		William McKinley becomes president of United States (Republican).
	George Bernard Shaw – *The Devil's Disciple*		National Union of Women's Suffrage Societies formed
	Marie Corelli – *Ziska*		Queen Victoria celebrates Diamond Jubilee.
	Bram Stoker – *Dracula*		Electrons are detected for first time by J. J. Thomson.
	H. G. Wells – *The Invisible Man*		
	William Morris – *The Sundering Flood* (published posthumously)		
1898	Henry James – *The Turn of the Screw*; *In the Cage* (novella)	Feminist Eleanor Marx dies	Spanish-American War begins.
	Joseph Conrad – *Tales of Unrest*	Olympic Games held in London	Ex-Liberal British prime minister William Gladstone dies.

Year	Select Literary Works	Cultural Events	Historical and Scientific Notes
	Arnold Bennett – *A Man From the North*		Cars first allowed on public roads in the United Kingdom
	Oscar Wilde – *The Ballad of Reading Gaol*		Rudolph Diesel demonstrates first internal combustion engine.
	Marie Corelli – *The Song of Miriam and Other Stories*		
	Ménie Muriel Dowie – *The Crook of the Bough*		
	H. G. Wells – *The War of the Worlds*		
1899	Kate Chopin – *The Awakening*	Publication of Arthur Symons's *The Symbolist Movement in Literature*	Boer War begins.
	Henry James – *The Awkward Age*		
	Margaret Oliphant – *Autobiography* (published posthumously)		
	George Bernard Shaw – *Caesar and Cleopatra*		
1900	Ellen Glasgow – *The Voice of the People*	Friedrich Nietzsche dies	British Labour Party founded, originally called Labour Representation Committee
	Henrik Ibsen – *When We Dead Awaken*	Oscar Wilde dies	Trial flight of the Zeppelin airship in Germany
	H. G. Wells – *Love and Mr. Lewisham*	W. B. Yeats – 'The Symbolism of Poetry'	(–1919) Max Planck proposes and works on quantum theory.
	Joseph Conrad – *Lord Jim*	Net Book Agreement between publishers and booksellers fixes prices for books	11 cities with populations over a million–London and New York over 5 million, Paris 3 million, Berlin 2 million

Continued

Year	Select Literary Works	Cultural Events	Historical and Scientific Notes
	Beatrix Potter – *The Tale of Peter Rabbit*	80 theatres on Broadway. London has 61 theatres by 1900.	Kodak Brownie Camera invented by Eastman.
	W. B. Yeats – *The Shadowy Waters* (play)	John Ruskin dies	From 1861, 7.5 million emigrate from the United Kingdom to Australia and New Zealand; 800,000 to Canada.
	Theodore Dreiser – *Sister Carrie*	Publication of Sigmund Freud's *The Interpretation of Dreams*	60 million people added to British Empire since 1870.
	Stephen Crane – *Whilomville Stories*		Universal Exhibition in Paris
	Oxford Book of English Verse 1250–1900 (edited by Arthur Quiller-Couch)		Rural population in the United Kingdom 8 per cent of total
	L. Frank Baum – *The Wonderful Wizard of Oz*		International Court of Justice founded. First named the Permanent Court of Arbitration.
			The United Kingdom's share of world's industrial output is 20 per cent (United States 30 per cent and Germany 17 per cent)
			Boxer risings in China
1901	Rudyard Kipling – *Kim*	The Oxford World's Classics series created	Queen Victoria dies, after more than 63 years on the throne.
	Ford Madox Ford and Joseph Conrad – *The Inheritors*	First awarding of Nobel Prize for Literature to Sully Prudhomme	Accession of Edward VII
	George Meredith – *A Reading of Life, with Other Poems*	Publication of Booker T. Washington's *Up from Slavery*	U.S. President McKinley assassinated. Replaced by Theodore Roosevelt (Republican).
	Miles Franklin – *My Brilliant Career*	Philosopher Friedrich Nietzsche's *The Will to Power* published posthumously	First transatlantic radio message sent by Marconi.

Year	Select Literary Works	Cultural Events	Historical and Scientific Notes
	Samuel Butler – *Erewhon Revisited*		Australia granted self-government with dominion status, with Edmund Barton as its first prime minister
1902	Joseph Conrad – 'Heart of Darkness' (first serialized in *Blackwood's Magazine* 1899) published in *Youth: A Narrative and Two Other Stories*	Émile Zola dies	Boer War ends, with 30,000 killed.
	Henry James – *The Wings of the Dove*	*Times Literary Supplement* launched	The Education Act abolishes School Boards and establishes Local Education Authorities.
	George Bernard Shaw – *Mrs. Warren's Profession* (written 1893)	Gustav Klimt – 'The Beethoven Frieze'	Arthur Balfour becomes British prime minister (Conservative).
	W. B. Yeats – *Cathleen ni Houlihan* (play)	Publication of Benedetto Croce's *Aesthetics as Science of Expression and General Linguistic*	Publication of Werner Sombart's *Modern Capitalism*. Concept of "modern capitalism" coined
	Arnold Bennett – *Anna of the Five Towns*		
	Rudyard Kipling – *Just So Stories*		
	August Strindberg – *A Dream Play*		
1903	Henry James – *The Ambassadors*	Publication of W. E. B. Du Bois's tract *The Souls of Black Folk*	Church attendance reduced by a quarter since 1886.
	Ford Madox Ford and Joseph Conrad – *Romance*	Philosopher Herbert Spencer dies	First air flight by Wright Brothers
	Joseph Conrad – *Typhoon and Other Stories*	(–1917) Alfred Stieglitz begins publishing journal *Camera Work,* in United States, site of photographic movement pictorialism	Women's Social and Political Union (Suffragettes) founded

Continued

TIMELINE

Year	Select Literary Works	Cultural Events	Historical and Scientific Notes
	Willa Cather – *April Twilights* (poetry)	Publication of Bertrand Russell's *Principles of Mathematics* Journal *Critica* founded and edited by Benedetto Croce	Ford Motor Company set up in the United States
1904	Henry James – *The Golden Bowl*	British newspaper *The Daily Mirror* regularly using photographs. (Founded by Lord Northcliffe in 1903)	United Kingdom and France sign *Entente Cordiale*.
	Joseph Conrad – *Nostromo*	Dublin's Abbey Theatre founded by W. B. Yeats, Edward Martyn and Lady Augusta Gregory	Russo-Japanese war begins.
	W. B. Yeats – *On Baile's Strand* (play); *In the Seven Woods*	Claude Monet – 'Houses of Parliament, London, Sun Breaking Through the Fog'	
	John Millington Synge – *Riders to the Sea*	Publication of Sigmund Freud's *Psychopathology of Everyday Life*	
	Anton Chekhov – *The Cherry Orchard* John Galsworthy – *The Island Pharisees*		
1905	Willa Cather – *The Troll Garden* (short stories)	Henri Matisse leads art exhibition in Paris with André Derain, beginning of the art movement fauvism	Albert Einstein conceives special theory of relativity
	George Bernard Shaw – *Man and Superman; Major Barbara*	Beginnings of the art movement expressionism	Sir Henry Campbell-Bannerman becomes British prime minister (Liberal).
	E. M. Forster – *Where Angels Fear to Tread*	Publication of Sigmund Freud's *Jokes and Their Relation to the Unconscious* and *Three Essays on the Theory of Sexuality*	Local tax revenue £108 million
	Edith Wharton – *The House of Mirth*	Publication of Benedetto Croce's *Logic*	*Sinn Féin* founded

Year	Select Literary Works	Cultural Events	Historical and Scientific Notes
	Jack London – *White Fang* Mark Twain – *King Leopold's Soliloquy* Arthur Conan Doyle – *The Return of Sherlock Holmes*		Petrol-driven tractors come into use. 'Revolution' in Russia – 'Bloody Sunday' Russo-Japanese war ends.
1906	John Galsworthy – *The Silver Box* (play); *The Man of Property* (first novel of the series *The Forsyte Saga*)	Paul Cézanne dies	Trade Disputes Act in the United Kingdom
	Upton Sinclair – *The Jungle*	The English Association founded	29 Labour MPs elected to Parliament.
1907	Joseph Conrad -*The Secret Agent*	Alfred Stieglitz takes famous photograph 'The Steerage'. (appears in *Camera Work 36* in 1911)	Policy of probation is introduced for offenders.
	John Millington Synge – *The Playboy of the Western World*	Friedrich Nietzsche's *Beyond Good and Evil* translated into English. (first published in German 1886)	Pope Pius X's encyclical *Pascendi Dominici Gregis* denounces modernism in Church
	E. M. Forster – *The Longest Journey*	Pablo Picasso – 'Les Demoiselles d'Avignon'	New Zealand and Newfoundland granted self-government with dominion status.
	Upton Sinclair – *The Overman*	Beginnings of cubist movement (Braque and Picasso)	*Triple Entente* signed (Russia, United Kingdom and France)
	Edith Wharton – *Madame de Treymes*		Second Hague Peace Conference
1908	Arnold Bennett – *The Old Wives' Tale*	(–1909) Ford Madox Ford edits *The English Review*; devoted to new experimental writing	Mass production of Ford Model T motor car in the United States
	E. M. Forster – *A Room with a View*	Publication of Henri Matisse's *Notes of a Painter*	Herbert Asquith becomes prime minister of the United Kingdom (Liberal).
	Joseph Conrad – *A Set of Six*		Introduction of old age pensions
	G. K. Chesterton – *The Man Who Was Thursday*		Austria-Hungary annexes Bosnia

Continued

Year	Select Literary Works	Cultural Events	Historical and Scientific Notes
1909	H. G. Wells – *Tono-Bungay*	Filippo Tommaso Marinetti publishes first futurist art manifesto *Le Figaro*	Blériot is first to fly across English Channel
	Gertrude Stein – *Three Lives*	Freud and Jung give first lectures on psychoanalysis in the United States at Clark University	Explorer Robert Peary reaches the North Pole.
	T. E. Hulme publishes first two imagist poems – 'Autumn' and 'A City Sunset' in Poet's Club Yearbook, *For Christmas MDCCCCVIII*	March – T. E. Hulme and F. S. Flint set up 'Secession Club', also called 'The School of Images'. Ezra Pound joins them (April). Other members are F. W. Tancred and Edward Storer	NAACP (National Association for the Advancement of Colored People) founded.
	John Galsworthy – *Strife* (play)	Publication of Roger Fry's 'An Essay in Aesthetics'	Nuclear physicist Ernest Rutherford splits the atom.
	L. Frank Baum – *The Road to Oz*		William H. Taft becomes president of United States (Republican).
1910	E. M. Forster – *Howards End*	Academic Committee founded, with purpose of finding best in English letters	George V becomes King of England after the death of Edward VII. Rules until 1936.
	H. G. Wells – *The History of Mr Polly*	International Psychoanalytical Association founded by Sigmund Freud and Carl Jung	Florence Nightingale dies at age 90 years.
	May Sinclair – *The Creators*	Postimpressionist exhibition of paintings, organized by Roger Fry, at Grafton Galleries, London	U.K. share of world trade falls from 25 per cent in 1870 to 14 per cent.
	John Galsworthy – *Justice*	(–1911) Wassily Kandinsky – 'Improvisations and Compositions' (non-figurative)	South Africa granted self-government with dominion status.

Year	Select Literary Works	Cultural Events	Historical and Scientific Notes
	Arnold Bennett – *Clayhanger*		Publication of Rudolf Hilferding's *Finance Capital: A Study of the Latest Phase of Capitalist Development* coins concept of 'finance capitalism.'
	George Bernard Shaw – *Misalliance*		W. E. B. Du Bois becomes editor of *The Crisis,* journal of the NAACP (National Association for the Advancement of Colored People)
1911	H. G. Wells – *The New Machiavelli*	Publication of Olive Schreiner's polemical history of women, *Women and Labour*	Explorer Amundsen reaches the South Pole.
	Joseph Conrad – *Under Western Eyes*	Publication of anthropologist Franz Boas' text on race, *The Mind of Primitive Man*	(–1912) Explorer Robert Falcon Scott reaches the South Pole, dies on return journey.
	Katherine Mansfield – *In a German Pension*	November – Publication of *The Freewoman* begins; periodical with a Feminist agenda	National Insurance Act passed in the United Kingdom; One of pre-cursors to welfare state.
	Dostoevsky's *Crime and Punishment* is translated into English by Constance Garnett	(–1912) Georges Braque – *The Portuguese*	Parliament Act stops the House of Lords' power of veto.
	Edith Wharton – *Ethan Frome*	Camden Town Group established, led by Walter Sickert. Introduced postimpressionism to Britain	
	E. M. Forster – *The Celestial Omnibus* (short stories)	Béla Bartók – *Bluebeard's Castle* (Opera)	
	D. H. Lawrence – *The White Peacock*		

Continued

Year	Select Literary Works	Cultural Events	Historical and Scientific Notes
1912	Willa Cather – *Alexander's Bridge*	James Rees Europe organizes 'Clef Club Orchestra' to play Carnegie Hall, first black ensemble at the venue	Dockers' and Miners' strikes
	Sui Sin Far (Edith Maude Eaton) – *Mrs. Spring* (one of the first Asian North American writers)	Chicago Renaissance begins. Represented by founding of two 'Little Magazines': *Poetry* and, in 1914, *The Little Review*	International Conference on Time in Paris establishes worldwide time system based on Greenwich mean time.
	James Weldon Johnson – *The Autobiography of an Ex-Coloured Man* (Republished at the peak of the Harlem Renaissance in 1927)	Ezra Pound names Hilda Doolittle and Richard Aldington 'imagistes', poems published in Harriet Monroe's *Poetry* (January 1913)	Home Rule Bill for Ireland
	Ezra Pound (ed.) – *Ripostes* (in which appeared the 'Complete Poetical Works of T. E. Hulme')	(–1913) Magazine *Poetry* launches imagist movement (U.S.)	*RMS Titanic*, largest steamship built, sinks; 1,513 lives lost.
	Arthur Conan Doyle – *The Lost World*	Chicago Little Theater founded	First International Air Exhibition takes place in Vienna.
	Joseph Conrad – *'Twixt Land and Sea* (includes 'The Secret Sharer')	Second postimpressionist exhibition held at Grafton Galleries, London; organized by Roger Fry	
	D. H. Lawrence – *The Trespasser*	Pablo Picasso conceives the 'collage'	
	(–1922) Edward Marsh (ed.) – *Georgian Poetry* (5 volumes)	Publication of Guillaume Apollinaire's *The Beginnings of Cubism*	
	Zane Grey – *Riders of the Purple Sage*	Jacob Epstein – "Tomb of Oscar Wilde"	
	Sir Arthur Conan Doyle – *The Lost World*	Posthumous publication of William James' *Essays in Radical Empiricism*	
	Sarah Grand – *Adnam's Orchard*	Publication of Sigmund Freud's *Totem and Taboo*	

Year	Select Literary Works	Cultural Events	Historical and Scientific Notes
1913	D. H. Lawrence – *Sons and Lovers*	Publication of Carl Jung's *The Psychology of the Unconscious* Dora Marsden and Harriet Shaw Weaver publish periodical *The New Freewoman*; new version of *The Freewoman*	First 'world time signal' from Greenwich
	(–1927) Marcel Proust – *In Search of Lost Time*	London Psychoanalytic Society founded by Ernest Jones	Niels Bohr discovers 'solar' atom.
	Joseph Conrad – *Chance*	Linguist Ferdinand De Saussure dies	Woodrow Wilson becomes president of United States (Democrat).
	Edith Wharton – *The Custom of the Country*	Publication of imagist manifesto 'Imagisme' by F. S. Flint	U.K. share of world's industrial output falls to 14 per cent (U.S. 36 per cent and Germany 16 per cent).
	Willa Cather – *O Pioneers!*	Publication of imagist manifesto 'A Few Don'ts by an Imagiste' by Ezra Pound	Air flights over 50 miles begin
	Robert Frost – *A Boy's Will*	Publication of the futurist's 'Manifesto' by F. T. Marinetti	Suffragette demonstrations held in London.
	George Bernard Shaw – *Pygmalion*	Poetry Bookshop (publishing company) founded by Harold Munro	Alfred North Whitehead and Bertrand Russell – *Principia Mathematica*
	Ellen Glasgow – *Virginia*	International Exhibition of Modern Art held in New York; (The Armory Show). Includes Marcel Duchamp's 'Nude Descending a Staircase'. Ernst Ludwig Kirchner – 'Berlin Street Scene' Marcel Duchamp – 'Bicycle Wheel' Jacob Epstein – 'Rock Drill'	

Continued

Year	Select Literary Works	Cultural Events	Historical and Scientific Notes
		(–1919) – Omega Workshops organized by Roger Fry London Group, of artists, founded Igor Stravinsky – *Rite of Spring* (Ballet)	
1914	James Joyce – *Dubliners*	*New Freewoman* renamed *The Egoist*	28 June – Assassination of Archduke Franz Ferdinand (heir to Austria-Hungarian throne)
	Ezra Pound (ed.) – *Des Imagistes* (poetry anthology)	Publication of futurist style 'Feminist Manifesto' by Mina Loy	First World War begins
	Gertrude Stein – *Tender Buttons* (poetry)	Publication *Blast* is launched, edited by Wyndham Lewis, 'First Vorticist Manifesto'	Civil servants employed by government number 200,000
	Robert Frost – *North of Boston*	T. E. Hulme gives his 'Lecture on Modern Poetry'	Church of England disestablished
	D. H. Lawrence – *The Prussian Officer and Other Stories*	Literary magazine *Little Review* launched by Margaret Anderson. (H.D., Richard Aldington, Amy Lowell and William Carlos Williams)	Conference on Home Rule for Ireland fails.
	Edgar Rice Burroughs – *Tarzan of the Apes*	(-January 1917) Edward Thomas writes 144 poems based on his experiences in First World War	
	Robert Tressell – *The Ragged Trousered Philanthropists*	Rebel Art Centre established; organized by Wyndham Lewis and Kate Lechmere	
	Carl Sandburg – *Chicago*	Henri Gaudier-Brzeska – '(Hieratic) Head of Ezra Pound' (–1915) Wyndham Lewis – 'The Crowd'	

Year	Select Literary Works	Cultural Events	Historical and Scientific Notes
1915	Virginia Woolf – *The Voyage Out*	Francis Picabia's illustrations: 'Portrait d'une jeune fille americaine' and 'Ici c'est ici Stieglitz: Foi et Amor' appear in *291* (U.S.)	Bulgaria enters First World War.
	D. H. Lawrence – *The Rainbow*	Publication of F. S. Flint's 'History of Imagism' in the *Egoist*	Herbert Asquith becomes British prime minister (Liberal, coalition government).
	(–1938) Dorothy Richardson – *Pilgrimage* (12 volumes)	*The Egoist* sells 1,250 copies of a special edition, 'Imagist' (normal circulation 750)	
	H. G. Wells – *Boon*	Provincetown Players founded in Massachusetts then New York. (beginning of New American Drama). Company was part of Little Theatre movement.	
	Ford Madox Ford – *The Good Soldier*	Rupert Brooke dies in First World War	
	Joseph Conrad – 'Within The Tides'; *Victory*	Ezra Pound embarks on writing narrative poem, *The Cantos*	
	(–1917) Amy Lowell – *Some Imagist Poets* (3 volume anthology)	(–1916) Helen Saunders – 'Abstract Multicoloured Design'	
	Willa Cather – *The Song of the Lark*	Vorticist exhibition held	
	Edgar Lee Masters – *Spoon River Anthology*	D. W. Griffith (dir.) – *Birth of a Nation* (U.S.)	
	Susan Glaspell – *Suppressed Desires*		
	Ezra Pound – *Cathay*		
	Richard Aldington – *Images: 1910–1915*		
	Franz Kafka – 'Metamorphosis'		
	Djuna Barnes – *The Book of Repulsive Women* (poetry and drawings)		

Continued

Year	Select Literary Works	Cultural Events	Historical and Scientific Notes
1916	James Joyce – *A Portrait of the Artist as a Young Man*	Ferdinand De Saussure's *Course in General Linguistics* translated into English	"Easter Rising" in Ireland
	Rose Macaulay – *Non-Combatants and Others*	Cabaret Voltaire set up in Zurich, signalling beginning of art movement Dadaism	David Lloyd George becomes British prime minister (Liberal, coalition government).
	Charlotte Mew – *The Farmer's Bride*	(–1921) Edith Sitwell begins editing annual anthology *Wheels*	First birth control clinic opened in the United States. Its owner, Margaret Sanger is prosecuted.
	Robert Frost – *Mountain Interval*	Max Ernst's 'Sturm Exhibition' held	
	(–1921) Edith Sitwell (ed.) – *Wheels* (poetry anthologies)		Romania enters First World War
	Susan Glaspell – *Trifles*		
	Robert Graves – *Over the Brazier*		
	H. D. (Hilda Doolittle) – *The Sea Garden*		
1917	Joseph Conrad – *The Shadow Line*	T. S. Eliot appointed assistant editor of *The Egoist*	Tsarist monarchy overthrown in Russia
	T. S. Eliot – *Prufrock and Other Observations*	Hogarth Press founded by Virginia and Leonard Woolf. Published 474 titles to 1941	Greece enters the First World War
	Siegfried Sassoon – *The Old Huntsman*	Original Dixieland Jazz Band records music, selling over one million copies	China enters the First World War.
	Virginia and Leonard Woolf – *Two Stories* published by Hogarth Press	Marcel Duchamp's famous readymade, "Fountain by R. Mutt," photographed by Alfred Stieglitz for *Blindman* (U.S.)	United States enters the First World War.
	Alice Meynell – *A Father of Women and Other Poems*	T. E. Hulme, one of the founders of the imagist movement in poetry, dies in First World War	Bolshevik Revolution in Russia, led by Vladimir Lenin, installs dictatorship.

TIMELINE

Year	Select Literary Works	Cultural Events	Historical and Scientific Notes
	Mina Loy – 'Songs to Johannes' (published in *Others*)	Edward Thomas dies in First World War	Russia ceases participation in First World War.
	Robert Graves – 'Goliath and David'; *Fairies and Fusiliers*	Exhibition of the vorticists held at the Penguin, New York	
	Harriet Monroe and Alice Corbin Henderson (eds.) – *The New Poetry: An Anthology*	Publication of May Sinclair's *A Defence of Idealism*	
	W. B. Yeats – *The Wild Swans at Coole*	Publication of Benedetto Croce's *The Theory of Historiography*	British capture Jerusalem.
1918	Rebecca West – *The Return of the Soldier*	Publication of imagist manifesto 'A Retrospect' by Ezra Pound	First World War ends with almost 10 million military deaths.
	James Joyce – *Exiles* (play)	*The Soldier's Tale* composed by Igor Stravinsky (musical)	Max Planck wins Nobel Prize for work on quantum theory.
	Wyndham Lewis – *Tarr*	The sales of the *Egoist* are down to 400 copies, with only 90 subscribers	Women over 30 years of age win right to vote in Great Britain.
	Willa Cather – *My Antonia*	Wilfred Owen dies in First World War	Russian Civil War begins
	Siegfried Sassoon – *Counter-Attack*	Publication of Lytton Strachey's history book, *Eminent Victorians*	Royal Air Force formed
	Booth Tarkington – *The Magnificent Ambersons*		School-leaving age raised to 14 years in the United Kingdom.
	Susan Glaspell – *Tickless Time*		Working week reduced from 56 to 48 hours in the United Kingdom.
	Lytton Strachey – *Eminent Victorians*		(–1919) Influenza pandemic (also known as Spanish flu) kills more people than the First World War (between 20 and 40 million people worldwide).

Continued

Year	Select Literary Works	Cultural Events	Historical and Scientific Notes
1919	May Sinclair – *Mary Olivier: A Life*	(–1920) Robert Wiene (dir.) – *The Cabinet of Dr Caligari* (Germany) Publication of Waldo Frank's manifesto for post–First World War American Nativists – *Our America*	Alcohol Prohibition becomes law in the United States. Pan-African Congress held in Paris.
	Virginia Woolf – *Night and Day*; 'Kew Gardens'; 'The Mark on the Wall'	Publication of T. S. Eliot's 'Tradition and the Individual Talent' in *The Egoist*	London-to-Paris regular flights begin.
	Sherwood Anderson – *Winesburg, Ohio*	Bauhaus, school of art and design, founded in Germany	Socialist state in Hungary is followed by counterrevolution six months later.
	Joseph Conrad – *The Arrow of Gold*; *Victory*	Pierre-Auguste Renoir dies	Albert Einstein conceives general theory of relativity.
	Robert Graves – *Treasure Box*	H. L. Mencken – *The American Language*	28 June – Treaty of Versailles signed; Germany ordered to pay large reparations.
	W. Somerset Maugham – *The Moon and Sixpence*	John Maynard Keynes – *The Economic Consequences of the Peace*	Nancy Astor becomes first woman MP elected to British parliament. Polish-Soviet war begins Left-wing uprising in Germany when Rosa Luxemburg is murdered. German Workers Party (GPW) founded in Munich.
1920	D. H. Lawrence – *Women in Love*; *The Lost Girl*	Publication of Roger Fry's essay collection *Vision and Design*	Typewriter invented by James Smathers.
	Katherine Mansfield – *Bliss, and Other Stories*	Publication of T. S. Eliot's essay collection *Sacred Wood*	Government in Ireland Act
	F. Scott Fitzgerald – *Flappers and Philosophers* (short stories); *This Side of Paradise*	Duncan Grant holds his first solo exhibition at the Carfax Gallery	Polish-Soviet war ends.

Year	Select Literary Works	Cultural Events	Historical and Scientific Notes
	Joseph Conrad – *The Rescue*	Publication of Georg Lukács's *The Theory of the Novel*	Ireland becomes an autonomous province of the United Kingdom.
	William Carlos Williams – *Kora in Hell*	Dadaist exhibition held at Winter Brewery, Cologne	GPW renamed National Socialist German Worker's Party (NSDAP.) or Nazi Party
	Willa Cather – *Youth and the Bright Medusa* (short stories)	Igor Stravinsky – *Pulcinella* (ballet)	Founding of the League of Nations. By December, there are 48 member states.
	Edith Wharton – *The Age of Innocence*		
	Eugene O'Neill – *The Emperor Jones*		
	Ezra Pound – *Hugh Selwyn Mauberley*		
1921	W. B. Yeats – *Michael Robartes and the Dancer*	Publication of D. H. Lawrence's *Psychoanalysis and the Unconscious*	Warren Harding becomes president of United States (Republican).
	Edwin Arlington Robinson – *Collected Poems*	The musical *Shuffle Along* becomes Broadway hit; first show exclusively created by African Americans.	Russian Civil War ends
	Susan Glaspell – *The Verge*	U. S. Supreme Court rules James Joyce's *Ulysses* breaches Obscenity Laws. The book is banned.	(–1922) – Washington Conference
	Aldous Huxley – *Crome Yellow*	Publication of Ludwig Wittgenstein's *Tractatus Logico-Philosophicus*	Washington Naval Agreement signed by United States, United Kingdom, Japan, France and Italy.
	H. D. (Hilda Doolittle) – *Hymen*		Anglo-Soviet Trade Treaty agreed.
	Virginia Woolf – *Monday or Tuesday*		Marie Stopes opens the United Kingdom's first birth control clinic.

Continued

Year	Select Literary Works	Cultural Events	Historical and Scientific Notes
	Marianne Moore – *Poems*		Adolf Hitler becomes the leader of the Nazi Party in Germany.
1922	James Joyce – *Ulysses*	F. W. Murnau (dir.) – *Nosferatu* (Germany)	Radio broadcasting begins in London.
	May Sinclair – *The Life and Death of Harriett Frean*	The literary journal *The Criterion* founded by T. S. Eliot	Andrew Bonar Law becomes prime minister of the United Kingdom (Conservative).
	Virginia Woolf – *Jacob's Room*	Edwin Arlington Robinson wins Pulitzer Prize for Poetry for *Collected Poems*	Irish Free State established
	Edith Sitwell – *Façade* (poem sequence)	*Vanity Fair* has circulation of 96,500 copies. (T. S. Eliot, D. H. Lawrence, and others)	December – Soviet Union (USSR) created.
	Rebecca West – *The Judge*	Publication of 'The Waste Land' in *Dial* (U.S.). This work wins Eliot the 'Dial Award', with $2000 prize.	1 November – Collapse of Ottoman Empire; Turkey declared a republic.
	December – T. S. Eliot – *The Waste Land*	Vanessa Bell holds first solo exhibition at Independent Gallery	German-Soviet Trade Treaty is signed.
	Katherine Mansfield – *The Garden Party and Other Stories*	Publication of James Weldon Johnson's *The Book of American Negro Poetry*	Benito Mussolini comes to power in Italy, signalling the beginning of a fascist dictatorship
	Claude McKay – *Harlem Shadows*	Surrealism founded as a movement, included artists André Breton and Salvador Dali	The British Broadcasting Corporation (BBC) founded.
	F. Scott Fitzgerald – *The Beautiful and Damned*	Publication of May Sinclair's *The New Idealism*	
	Willa Cather – *One of Ours*	Publication of Bronislaw Malinowski's *Argonauts of the Western Pacific* (ethnography)	

Year	Select Literary Works	Cultural Events	Historical and Scientific Notes
	Bertolt Brecht – *Drums in the Night* Eugene O'Neill – *The Hairy Ape* D. H. Lawrence – *Aaron's Rod*; *England, My England and other stories*		
1923	Rose Macaulay – *Told by an Idiot*	The Broadway show *Shuffle Along* tours Europe	Werner Heisenberg conceives uncertainty principle (physics).
	Jean Toomer – *Cane*	Publication of Roger Fry's *The Sampler of Castile*	Stanley Baldwin becomes British prime minister (Conservative).
	Aldous Huxley – *Antic Hay*	Publication of Sigmund Freud's *The Ego and the Id*	Calvin Coolidge becomes president of United States (Republican).
	Wallace Stevens – *Harmonium*	First FA Cup Final played at Wembley between Bolton and West Ham. 200,000 people attend	
	E. E. Cummings – *Tulips and Chimneys* Djuna Barnes – *A Book* (–1925) Mina Loy – 'Anglo-Mongrels and the Rose' (published in *The Little Review*); *Lunar Baedecker* William Carlos Williams – *Spring and All* Robert Frost – *New Hampshire* Bertolt Brecht – *Baal* Joseph Conrad – *The Rover* D. H. Lawrence – *Kangaroo*; *The Ladybird, the Fox, the Captain's doll* (short stories)		

Continued

Year	Select Literary Works	Cultural Events	Historical and Scientific Notes
1924	E. M. Forster – *A Passage to India*	Sergei Eisenstein (dir.) – *Strike* (U.S.S.R.)	James Ramsey MacDonald becomes British prime minister for ten months (Labour), followed by Stanley Baldwin (Conservative).
	(–1928) Ford Madox Ford – *Parade's End* (novel tetralogy)	Paul Whiteman holds musical recital, 'An Experiment in Modern Music', in New York	Dawes Plan reschedules Germany's reparations.
	Bertolt Brecht – *Edward II*	Publication of T. E. Hulme's writings, *Speculations* (Herbert Read ed.)	Vladimir Lenin, leader of the USSR, dies.
	Eugene O'Neill – *Desire Under the Elms*	Publication of André Breton's 'First Manifesto of Surrealism', originally to be the introduction to *Poisson Soluble*	
	H. D. (Hilda Doolittle) – *Heliodora and Other Poems*	Claude Monet dies	
	D. H. Lawrence – *The Boy in the Bush*	Fernand Léger and Dudley Murphy (dirs.) – *Ballet Mécanique* (Dadaist film – France)	
	Marianne Moore – *Observations*		
	Thomas Mann – *The Magic Mountain*		
1925	Virginia Woolf – *Mrs. Dalloway*	Sergei Eisenstein (dir.) – *Battleship Potemkin* (U.S.S.R.)	Plaid Cymru formed (Welsh National Party).
	Joseph Conrad – *Tales of Hearsay* (published posthumously)	November – Premiere of Aaron Copland's jazz-based composition 'Music for the Theatre' (U.S.)	German chemical industry merges to form IG Farbenindustrie.
	Franz Kafka – *The Trial* (published posthumously)	Publication of Virginia Woolf's collection of essays, *The Common Reader*	'New Household' exhibition held in Vienna, showcasing electrical household items (not a reality for most citizens for another 30 years).

Year	Select Literary Works	Cultural Events	Historical and Scientific Notes
	Nancy Cunard – *Parallax* (long poem published by Virginia Woolf's 'Hogarth Press')	Publication of I. A. Richards's *Principles of Literary Criticism*	
	Sherwood Anderson – *Dark Laughter*	Sigmund Freud's *Collected Papers* are published in English by the Hogarth Press	
	Alain Locke (ed.) – *The New Negro* (anthology)	Publication of Viktor Shklovsky's *Poetics of Prose* (Russian formalism)	
	Sylvia Townsend Warner – *The Espalier*	Charlie Chaplin (dir.) – *The Gold Rush* (U.S.)	
	Ernest Hemingway – *In Our Time*		
	W. B. Yeats – *A Vision*		
	F. Scott Fitzgerald – *The Great Gatsby*		
	William Carlos Williams – *In the American Grain*		
	H. D. (Hilda Doolittle) – *Collected Poems*		
	Ezra Pound – *A Draft of XVI Cantos* (First section of the poem. Poem incomplete at time of death in November 1972, although fragments published 1969)		
	D. H. Lawrence – *St. Mawr*		
	E. E. Cummings – *&; XLI Poems*		
	Aldous Huxley – *Those Barren Leaves*		
	Ellen Glasgow – *Barren Ground*		
	Gertrude Stein – *The Making of Americans*		
	Countee Cullen – *Color*		
1926	Sylvia Townsend Warner – *Lolly Willowes or the Loving Huntsman*	Fritz Lang (dir.) – *Metropolis* (Germany)	The rocket developed by Robert Goddard.

Continued

Year	Select Literary Works	Cultural Events	Historical and Scientific Notes
	Franz Kafka – *The Castle*	Publication of Wyndham Lewis's *The Art of Being Ruled* (philosophy)	BBC becomes government owned.
	Ezra Pound – *Personae*	London Artists Association formed, and first exhibition held	Germany joins League of Nations.
	Langston Hughes – *The Weary Blues*		The television is invented.
	Olive Schreiner – *From Man to Man* (novel published posthumously)		General Strike in the United Kingdom
	Vita Sackville-West – *The Land*		The United Kingdom's chemical industry merges to form Imperial Chemical Industries.
	Ernest Hemingway – *The Sun Also Rises*		
	Hart Crane – *White Buildings*		
	D. H. Lawrence – *The Plumed Serpent*; *Sun* (short stories)		
	F. Scott Fitzgerald – *All the Sad Young Men*		
	William Faulkner – *Soldiers' Pay*		
	Richard Aldington – *The Love of Myrrhine and Konallis, and Other Prose Poems*		
	T. E. Lawrence – *The Seven Pillars of Wisdom: A Triumph* (memoir)		
1927	Virginia Woolf – *To The Lighthouse*	Publication of E. M. Forster's critical text *Aspects of the Novel*	League of Nations holds International Economic Conference in Geneva. First discussion of the problem of cartels on an international forum.

Year	Select Literary Works	Cultural Events	Historical and Scientific Notes
	Ernest Hemingway – *Men Without Women*	Publication of Wyndham Lewis's *Time and Western Man* (philosophy)	
	Sylvia Townsend Warner – *Mr. Fortune's Maggot*	Premiere of Aaron Copland's musical composition 'Piano Concerto'	
	Countee Cullen – *Copper Sun*	George Antheil's 'Ballet Mécanique' (originally a film score) and 'Jazz Symphony' performed at Carnegie Hall (U.S.)	
	William Faulkner – *Mosquitoes*	Publication of Robert Graves and Laura Riding's *A Survey of Modernist Poetry*	
	Herman Hesse – *Steppenwolf*	Publication of Martin Heidegger's *Being and Time*	
	Jean Rhys – *The Left Bank*	Walther Ruttmann (dir.) – *Berlin: Symphony of a Great City* (Germany)	
		F. W. Murnau (dir.) – *Sunrise: A Song of Two Humans* (Germany)	
1928	D. H. Lawrence – *Lady Chatterley's Lover*	Thomas Hardy dies	Women between ages of 21 and 30 win vote in Great Britain.
	W. B. Yeats – *The Tower*	Luis Buñuel and Salvador Dali (dirs.) *Un Chien andalou* (France)	Discovery of penicillin by Alexander Fleming
	Virginia Woolf – *Orlando: A Biography*	Sergei Eisenstein (dir.) – *October (Ten Days That Shook The World)* (U.S.S.R.)	Publication of A. S. Eddington's *The Nature of the Physical World*
	Nella Larsen – *Quicksand*	Publication of Ray Strachey's *The Cause: A Short History of the Women's Movement in Great Britain*	Scottish National Party formed.
	Aldous Huxley – *Point Counter Point*	Publication of Edmund Blunden's war memoir, *Undertones of War*	Briand-Kellogg Pact renounces war. Signed by 64 countries.

Continued

Year	Select Literary Works	Cultural Events	Historical and Scientific Notes
	Christopher Isherwood – *All the Conspirators*	Publication of André Breton's novel/ photographic essay *Nadja*	Emmeline Pankhurst, prominent suffragette, dies.
	Wyndham Lewis – *The Childermass*	Publication of Radclyffe Hall's *The Well of Loneliness* causes largest censorship case in United Kingdom	(–1932) – first of the USSR's Five-Year Plans aims to increase productivity of labour and economic growth.
	W. E. B. Du Bois – *Dark Princess* (novel)	Carl Theodore Dreyer (dir.) – *Passion of Joan of Arc* (France)	.
	Jean Rhys – *Quartet*	Dziga Vertov (dir.) – *Man with a Movie Camera* (U.S.S.R.)	
	Evelyn Waugh – *Decline and Fall*		
	Robert Frost – *West-Running Brook*		
	Eugene O'Neill – *Strange Interlude*		
	Siegfried Sassoon – *Memoirs of a Fox-Hunting Man* (fictional memoir)		
	E. M. Forster – *The Eternal Moment* (short stories)		
	Sylvia Townsend Warner – *Time Importuned*		
	Claude McKay – *Home to Harlem*		
	Djuna Barnes – *Ladies Almanack*; *Ryder*		
1929	Rebecca West – *Harriet Hume*	Publication of Virginia Woolf's *A Room of One's Own*	24 October – 'The Wall Street Crash', beginning of Great Depression (U.S.)
	Nella Larsen – *Passing*	Publication of Walter Benjamin's 'Surrealism: The Last Snapshot of the European Intelligentsia'	James Ramsay MacDonald reelected as British prime minister (Labour).
	William Faulkner – *The Sound and the Fury*		Joseph Stalin comes to power in the USSR.

Year	Select Literary Works	Cultural Events	Historical and Scientific Notes
	Richard Aldington – *Death of a Hero*		Young Plan increases Germany's reparations once again.
	Sylvia Townsend Warner – *The True Heart*		The Vatican State comes into being in Italy.
	Ernest Hemingway – *A Farewell to Arms*		Establishment of the Kingdom of Yugoslavia combines Serb, Croat and Slovene nations.
	Edith Sitwell – *Gold Coast Customs*		The UnitedKingdom's share of world industrial output falls to 9 per cent (United States 42 per cent and Germany 12 per cent).
	Charlotte Mew – *The Rambling Sailor*		
	Elizabeth Bowen – *The Last September*		
1930	William Faulkner – *As I Lay Dying*	Luis Buñuel and Salvador Dali (Dirs.) – *L'Âge d'or* (France)	Publication of James Jean's *The Mysterious Universe*
	Wyndham Lewis – *The Apes of God*	Publication of last *Imagist Anthology*	Herbert Hoover becomes president of the United States (Republican).
	John Dos Passos – *The 42nd Parallel* (first novel in U.S. trilogy)	Publication of William Empson's *Seven Types of Ambiguity*	Germany's President Hindenberg activates Article 48 of the Weimar Constitution, signalling the beginning of the end of democracy in Germany.
	Evelyn Waugh – *Vile Bodies*	Béla Bartók – *Cantata Profana* (choral work)	
	Hart Crane – *The Bridge*	Publication of Sigmund Freud's *Civilisation and its Discontents*	

INTRODUCTION: BEFORE THE 1900s

In his essay 'When Was Modernism?' Raymond Williams observed that the answer to this question is a matter of 'selective tradition' (Williams: 31). Most discussions of modernism in English concentrate on the first decades of the twentieth century, as will the present study. However, in the Conclusion I will look at Anglophone modernism after 1930 and beyond Anglo-America, and in this Introduction I identify some of the writers, ideas and practices that paved the way for writers commonly identified as 'modernists' and who also have a part to play in most outlines of 'what modernism was'.

While modernism is associated with the twentieth century in Anglophone countries, its main roots lie in the nineteenth century and others stretch farther back. From the perspective of the twenty-first century, there are also many constructions and opinions of different modernisms that intercede between a reader and the texts that have had the label modernist attached to them. Literary 'modernism' arose as a convenient term to encompass a number of both interlinked and discrete avant-garde works that were attempting to move against a dominant current, to write against a grain of thought, practice, or formal convention that seemed limiting in literature or life. Modernism can therefore be thought of as an impulse to reshape literature and expand the borders of the possible in written language, to break out of prisons of referentiality constructed by writing traditions of the past. It is also a term that has hardened around certain writers and texts who aspired to this agenda of remaking, and who have been studied, taught, or presented together for the purposes of writing literary history.

What modernism does not cover is, for the most part, more contentious than what it does. This is the case in terms of both writers and periods. There are some authors who are closely associated with modernism, such as T. S. Eliot, Virginia Woolf, Ezra Pound and James Joyce, though Woolf would not always have been present on this list. Whether writers as varied as D. H. Lawrence, Jean Rhys, Elizabeth Bowen, Ernest Hemingway and George Orwell should be discussed under a heading of modernist writing has been the subject of much argument, and most critics would have decided views about each author. This is not just about the aesthetics, but also the *politics* of modernism, which is a subject Raymond Williams considered in his book of that name. His reading is partly focused on the ways in which a radical, avant-garde approach to writing became a bastion of conservatism in critical circles as a canon of modernism evolved in the 1950s and 1960s. Other political aspects to modernism embrace the exclusion of women writers (Dorothy Richardson, May Sinclair, Charlotte Mew, Rebecca West, Mina Loy, Edith Sitwell, and many more) from masculinist accounts of modernism. In terms of class, debates often revolve around a writer like D. H. Lawrence, alongside accusations of misogyny developed after Simone De Beauvoir's reading of him in *The Second Sex*. But modernism is not itself rife with texts that consider matters of class, and class consciousness is more explicitly addressed in a text such as *The Ragged Trousered Philanthropists* (1914) by Robert Tressell, which is not an experimental work, but one which dramatized Marxist socialism to a wider working-class audience than any other novel did. From another political angle, the difficulty and complexity of modernism, along with the espousal of right-wing causes by several of its most prominent writers, have led to accusations that range from elitism to an inbred conservatism and a pronounced leaning towards fascism.

Modernism was an international movement, largely originating in Europe, but one immersed in international arts and culture more generally. Anglophone writers took to avant-garde work later and less radically, for the most part, than authors in other languages. British modernism was also enriched by migrant writers arriving from the European Continent, the United States and elsewhere, alongside cultural artefacts brought to the British Imperial hub of London from around the world. This is a subject I take up again in the Conclusion.

Dates are often attached to modernism in an attempt to delimit and to historicize the writings that fall under this heading. In Anglo-American literature, these attempts usually contain, but may move before or after, the three decades principally treated in this book, from 1900 to 1929. This is the period of what we might call 'classic modernism' in the same way that texts of a preceding 'classic realism' have been anatomized by critics such as Colin MacCabe and Catherine Belsey; but realism is not circumscribed by the techniques of Balzac and George Eliot, nor is modernism by the writings of Joyce and Woolf. Modernism hinges on the first decades of the twentieth century in the sense that this has been the period of main critical focus, but it spreads far wider. Attempts at periodization can also give way to a sense instead of a 'way of knowing' that was simply at its zenith in a certain period of history. To which point, it must also be added that while modernist writing was most prevalent in the period from 1900 to 1929, it was in no way pervasive. Quite the contrary, in fact: modernism was a minority interest in terms of both writers and readers, and it is only critical opinion that has given it continued currency and cultural capital. Modernism in the second half of the twentieth century thus came to occupy a place of cultural dominance far in excess of its popularity and signally against the countercultural position it occupied when practised by writers who espoused the avant-garde.

Modernism, in part, grew out of the movements of the late nineteenth century that wished to establish literature as art. Such movements as aestheticism, symbolism and naturalism inclined toward the self-reflexive, contemplative, refined image of the author, as opposed to a perceived rising tide of professionals, journalists, and populist writers. Alongside the spread of literacy accompanying mass education, there was a growth in mass market periodicals, low-cost book series, illustrated periodicals, and best-selling newspapers like *The Daily Mail*, and also a 'New Woman' print culture resulting from a dissatisfaction with women's traditional roles in society. The origins of modernism existed in the activities of those who sought a countermovement in a distinctly 'literary' space, in impressionism, short stories and one-act plays, 'decadent' aestheticist publications like the 1890s quarterly *The Yellow Book*, intellectual political and philosophical stances, societies of authors, international influences and technical innovations.

In the English-language novel, Henry James had established in the 1880s that fiction could be an art form alongside poetry, music and painting. Taking a cue from European writers, and Flaubert in particular, his essay 'The Art of Fiction' (1884) is perhaps the foundational critical text that makes the case for the aesthetic status of the novelist's architectural re-creation of mental consciousness in a house of fiction. Seeing the novel as a personal image of life, James developed a dense, detailed style that located fine sensibilities in the intricate workings of characters' thoughts, rendered in complex, clause-laden, labyrinthine prose. In this, James both established the principle of attention to language as the primary purpose of the novelist's art and the pursuit of an individual style as the essence of modernism, which is, for the most part, a grouping of very different, individualistic and idiosyncratic but ground-breaking writers.

In poetry, the French examples of writers such as Baudelaire and Verlaine pointed in experimental directions, but there were many English-language proponents of experimental verse, from Emily Dickinson and Walt Whitman in the United States, to Gerard Manley Hopkins and the symbolist Arthur Symons in Britain. Writers like Oscar Wilde and Robert Browning also explored aspects of writing that would be mined by modernist authors, from the poetry of prose to the analysis of self.

Tending to associate art with a freedom from traditional genre and form, modernist literature is self-consciously experimental and formally complex, seeing language as a substance and identity as rooted in cultural dislocation. Beyond this, there are several modernisms in the intensifying sequence of art movements named symbolism, postimpressionism, expressionism, futurism, imagism, vorticism, Dadaism, surrealism, and so on. These are often also radically at odds, such that the post-symbolist stress on the 'hard' or impersonal image within Imagism can liquefy into the fluidity of Dada or surrealism, all qualified by a full spectrum of political attitudes and forms of historicism.

I want to end this Introduction by looking at the pre-1900 work of the author who will be the first novelist examined in the main body of this study: Joseph Conrad. The author of 31 books and numerous stories, Conrad is noted for complex narratives and formal experiments, especially in terms of point of view and temporal shifts. He is also much studied for his depiction of imperialism and colonialism: in the Malay Archipelago in *Almayer's Folly* (1895), *An Outcast of the Islands* (1896) and others; in the Belgian Congo in *Heart of Darkness* (1899; book publication 1902); and in South America in *Nostromo* (1904).

An only child, Conrad was born in Russian Poland on December 3, 1857, the year of Flaubert's seminal *Madame Bovary* and of the Indian 'Mutiny'. Unhappy at school, Conrad was enthralled by the sea from an early age and joined the French merchant navy in 1874, becoming an ordinary sailor, much to the displeasure of his family, who considered this a rejection of his social and national roots. In 1878, he switched to an English ship, and became a British subject in 1886, teaching himself the new language. Until he was 21, Conrad had never set foot in England, and it was only his transfer to the British merchant navy that led to his becoming an *English* novelist. Conrad may thus stand as a signal modernist, in that he wrote in English, but this was not his first language; he was an émigré to Britain and later a nationalized British citizen. His example can suggest the international, cosmopolitan aspect of literary modernism.

In his career at sea, Conrad ascended from ordinary seaman to captain, and visited South America, Central Africa, India, Australia and the Far East. He started writing around 1886, but his first novel, *Almayer's Folly*, was not published until a decade later. His imperial adventure fiction appealed to a generation of readers who were soon to make Kipling the most successful fiction writer in the world, but Conrad's emphasis on psychological realism and his extensive use of indirect narration from multiple viewpoints were major stumbling blocks to wide commercial acceptance.

Having captained his first ship in 1888, Conrad took command in 1890 of a stern-wheel steamboat on the Congo River. He was working for a Belgian company charged by its owner, King Léopold II, with exploiting the country. After a journey of a thousand miles he reached Stanley Falls. Here he found what he called the 'vilest scramble for loot' in all of history, and the experience informed both one of his best short stories, 'An Outpost of Progress' (in *Tales of Unrest*), and his best-known work, *Heart of Darkness*. The trip also took its toll on Conrad's health and on his outlook, which became gloomier. In 1894, Conrad found himself with time on his hands when the ship he was to join as second mate had its voyage cancelled. He used this opportunity, after five years, to finally finish *Almayer's Folly*, which was accepted by Fisher Unwin in October 1894. One of Unwin's readers for the book was Edward Garnett, who was to become a valuable correspondent and editor over the coming years (and not just to Conrad; among others, D. H. Lawrence and John Galsworthy, a friend of Conrad's since 1891, were also nurtured by Garnett).

The critical reception of *Almayer's Folly*, a story of treasure, smuggling and miscegenation in Borneo, was mixed, with one critic in the *Spectator* observing that Conrad might become the Kipling of the Malay Archipelago. However, the book's literary merits were widely agreed upon, and Conrad was sufficiently pleased with reviews to continue writing.

His next year was spent writing *An Outcast of the Islands* (1896) – in many ways a novel similar to his first – and the stories that would go into *Tales of Unrest* (1898); but Conrad was in many ways searching around for a new direction while making a number of false starts.

This new direction came with his short third novel *The Nigger of the 'Narcissus'* (1897), which concerns a ship caught in a storm on its journey from Bombay to London. Overall, the book draws a stark contrast between the individualist ethic of the younger crew and the single-minded involvement in collective endeavour of the practical older sailors, who embody the qualities Conrad admires, such as dedication, perseverance, and application. For Conrad, the novel concerned a group of men held together by a 'common loyalty' in hostile conditions that would test to the limit their strength of purpose in their calling as seamen. It is thus a story of mutual dependency as much as potential mutiny. The central figure in this crucible of emotion in the ship's forecastle is the eponymous James Wait, who Conrad called 'the centre of the ship's collective psychology'. Complementary to this focus on both the individual and the collective, Conrad's novel uses both a third-person omniscient narrator and a first-person narrator, one of the crew. He has, however, been criticized for failing to maintain a consistent narrative point of view in the story, evident, for example, in the many changes from 'I' to 'we' to 'they'.

Most of Conrad's books were serialized, meaning he was paid a second time for the work when a novel was published, but he still suffered financially. Of material and artistic help to him were his firm friendships, dating from around this time, with several leading writers, such as Cunninghame Graham, Stephen Crane and Ford Madox Ford (then Hueffer). As was typical of authors within the networks that allowed modernism to flourish, he also got to know many of the literary giants of the day, including H. G. Wells, Henry James and George Bernard Shaw. James wrote to Edmund Gosse in a letter of 1902 that *The Nigger of the 'Narcissus'* was 'the masterpiece' of English writing about the sea and life at sea. However, perhaps the most quoted part of the book is a section of Conrad's Author's Note, which appeared after the final serial instalment and in which he wrote that his task was 'by the power of the written word, to make you hear, to make you feel – it is, before all, to make you *see*.' Conrad thus aspired in his writing more to painting than to music, often considered the purest of the arts. He had inherited the Flaubertian ideal of precision and verisimilitude, but transmuted these principles into a more symbolic and impressionistic form of writing. Most famously, he began his Author's Note by saying that

> Any work that aspires, however humbly, to the condition of art should carry its justification in every line. And art itself may be defined as a single-minded attempt to render the highest kind of justice to the visible universe, by bringing to light the truth, manifold and one, underlying its every aspect. It is an attempt to find in its forms, in its colours, in its light, in its shadows, in the aspects of matter, and in the facts of life what of each is fundamental, what is enduring and essential – their one illuminating and convincing quality – the very truth of their existence. (Conrad 1963a: Author's Note)

The Nigger of the 'Narcissus', with its shifting narrative perspectives and its use of repeating imagery, might thus be seen as chiefly important in its transitional status, situated between the emphases of realist writing, especially on plot, and the shifted perspectives of modernist prose, more concerned with formal properties and symmetrical designs, as well as less concerned with plot than character. His first major work, its standing in Conrad's *oeuvre* is fairly high, though it is less studied than the acknowledged masterpieces, beginning with *Heart of Darkness*, which more clearly express the preoccupations of modernism, such as a solipsistic mental landscape, an unreliable narrator, psychological and linguistic repetition, an obsession with language and imagery, a questioning of 'reality', uncertainty in a Godless universe, and the constraints of society against the drives of passion. These, together with critiques of Victorian and nineteenth-century habits of thought and expression, will recur in the analyses that follow, which will take a broadly chronological approach to nearly 50 of the defining texts and authors most commonly discussed under the heading 'modernist literature'.

CHAPTER ONE

1900s

INTRODUCTION

Whereas in the United States the decade is marked by the Presidency of Theodore Roosevelt (1901–1909), in Britain the 1900s are bounded by the accession of Edward VII at the start of the century and the accession of George V in 1910. While the passing of the century had been characterized by fin de siècle decadence on the one hand, and progressive social and technological hopes on the other, Queen Victoria's death in 1901 brought an end to a sixty-year reign. H. G. Wells wrote that 'Victoria sat on England like a great paper-weight and that after her death things blew about all over the place' (Millard: 2). According to W. B. Yeats's, writing in the *Oxford Book of English Verse* 'in 1900 everybody got down off his stilts ... Victorianism had been defeated' (Yeats 1936: xi–xii). This was, however, a time of Imperial pride but also uncertainty, as the expanding British Empire was becoming a financial burden and the Boer War (1899–1902) proved that empires could be outfought by guerrilla tactics. The opening years of the century were also a period of state expansion as legislation affecting poverty, unemployment, and the vote contributed to the idea that people could and should be administered, managed and policed. This development was necessary due to the pressure of mass enfranchisement, state control and social responsibility, but also in several respects a working through of the late nineteenth-century interest in Social Darwinism, the theory that cultures and civilizations might actually develop in ways that parallel the evolution of species, such that the most successful peoples would be those best adapted to changing conditions.

Literature from 1900 to 1914 was also often concerned with issues of social identity and national pride: it is in part this focus that causes it to stand out as a particular period. Samuel Hynes argues that 'the time between the turn of the century and the First World War does seem to have the qualities that make a literary period' including 'a consciousness of its own separateness from what went before and what followed, and a body of literature that expresses that consciousness' (Hynes 1972: 1). Given that the poetry of the period is almost uniformly considered to be poor, that body of literature would be discussed in terms of drama and particularly fiction, from Edith Wharton to Arthur Conan Doyle, Upton Sinclair to Jack London. This was the time of Barrie's *Peter Pan* and Grahame's *The Wind in the Willows*, of Kipling's *Puck of Pook's Hill* and H. G. Wells's condition-of-England novels such as *The History of Mr Polly* and *Tono-Bungay*. In all these works, the concrete encroachments of the cities are contrasted with an endangered but perennial, idyllic rural England. This national sense of threat and loss is also there in poetry, where the change is perhaps best seen in terms of the death of certain figures. Although other well-established writers were to live well into the twentieth century, Matthew Arnold had died in 1888, Robert Browning in 1889, Walt Whitman and Tennyson in 1892. Dante and Christina Rossetti were also both dead by 1894. A new vanguard was expected to emerge at this momentous point in history and in literature, yet the enormously popular poets that came to the fore were those who merely wished to celebrate the past and their own relation to it. The poets of 1901 to 1910 were deeply conscious of all that had gone before them; concerned with the veneration of an existing order, their poetry was, for the most part, patriotic, conservative, imperialistic and imitative. For example, there was the now little known Poet Laureate from 1896 to 1913, Alfred Austin, a prominent Tory journalist who stood twice for Parliament and proclaimed the glories of England. His poems have titles such as 'In Praise of England' 'On Returning to England' and 'Why England is Conservative'. Only the late poetry of Hardy and the uniformly excellent Edward Thomas provide much sense of literary value in retrospect. Against such a vision we need to place a rival view: that of the decadent poets of the 1890s, such as Ernest Dowson and Arthur Symons. The emphasis of these London avant-garde aesthetes, most widely celebrated in the work of Oscar Wilde, who himself died in 1900, was on style and sensation – not on the meaning of experiences, but their intensity and sweetness. It is the Decadents who, in the face of nationalist, masculinist and collectivist discourses, championed the values of the individual and offered a challenge to the dominant sexual and social attitudes of the time, influencing the internationalism and experimentation of modernism. The Decadents proposed the kind of 'art for art's sake' revolution that might have led to similarly significant changes in British aesthetics and to the many contemporary advances in science and engineering.

In the arts, despite the efforts of Jacob Epstein, T. S. Eliot, Ezra Pound, Wyndham Lewis and D. H. Lawrence, the force of modernism would not be greatly felt until after the war. In the United States, key works of nonfiction and fiction were published in the 1900s, particularly those challenging accepted views of race, in Booker T. Washington's *Up From Slavery* and W. E. B. DuBois's *Souls of Black Folk* (1903) and of gender, in Theodore Dreiser's *Sister Carrie* (1900) and Edith Wharton's *The House of Mirth* (1905). Meanwhile, abroad, Franz Kafka was writing *The Trial* and Marcel Proust *In Remembrance of Things Past*. Baudelaire, Mallarmé, Verlaine and Rimbaud had already transformed French poetry. In fine art, Picasso, Braque, Duchamp and others were overturning the fundamental principles of representation and perspective. The first London post-impressionist exhibition stunned the English in 1910, while in Paris two years later there was already the first futurist exhibition. The United States was famously introduced to avant-garde art in 1913 at the International Exhibition of Modern Art held in New York (The Armory Show). Schoenberg's first atonal work was produced in 1909 and Stravinsky's *Rite of Spring* was performed four years later.

Britain and British literature seemed preoccupied with the past, in comparison with most of the rest of Europe and America. Samuel Hynes characterizes the beginning of the Edwardian period in terms of sombre moods, melancholy and nostalgia: the end of a century, the death of a monarch whose predecessor few were old enough to remember, the culmination of an economic and social revolution of living patterns. The Edwardians, he says, were conscious of living in a period of transition, of having left late romantic Victorian poetry behind, but having travelled nowhere new. The century had started inauspiciously, leaving T. S. Eliot to conclude 'In the first decade of the century the situation was unusual. I cannot think of a single living poet, either in England or America, then at the height of his powers, whose work was capable of pointing the way to a young poet conscious of the desire for a new idiom' (Hynes 1972: 9).

HEART OF DARKNESS (1902) AND THE CONGO

In the late nineteenth century, Africa was subject to increasing European interest as its mineral and other resources came to be better appreciated. As a result, the Berlin Conference of 1884–5 established the formal international legitimacy of European claims, while the Act that issued from it became the authorizing document of the 'scramble for Africa'. One judgement in particular proved highly contentious. This was the decision to make the Congo the sole property of the King of Belgium. According to King Léopold II of Belgium, in his welcoming speech to the Geographical Conference in Brussels in September 1876, his aim was 'a crusade worthy of this century of progress': 'To open up to civilization the only part of our globe which it has not yet penetrated, to pierce the darkness which hangs over entire peoples.' The result, however, was described by Arthur Conan Doyle in these words: 'Had the nations gathered round been able to perceive its [the Belgian Congo's] future, the betrayal of religion and civilization of which it would be guilty, the immense series of crimes which it would perpetrate throughout central Africa, the lowering of the prestige of all the white races, they would surely have strangled the monster in its cradle.' (Doyle: 7) Doyle went on to base characters in his 1912 adventure novel *The Lost World* on human rights campaigners E. D. Morel and Roger Casement, who protested against the regime in the Congo. In the year before he published *The Lost World*, he wrote his tract *The Crime of the Congo*, from which the above words are taken, to bring to world attention the atrocities committed against Africans in their country and the work of the Congo Reform Association. Doyle also argued from a political standpoint that if France were to ally itself with King Léopold, it would put its *entente cordiale* with Britain at risk. Doyle described the system at work in the Congo Free State as 'the greatest crime in all history' (Doyle: 87). Meanwhile, in the United States, Mark Twain published his pamphlet 'King Léopold's Soliloquy' in 1905, an attack in the form of a political satire in which Léopold defends himself lamentably against his critics.

A more famous and earlier literary response is Joseph Conrad's *Heart of Darkness*. Conrad's novella was serialized in 1899 in *Blackwood's Magazine*, but was not published in book form until its inclusion in *Youth, A Narrative, and Two Other Stories* in 1902. For some critics, it is the first important modernist work written in English. The book is divided into three chapters that follow a journey by Charles Marlow along the river Congo to find a man called Kurtz, who is positioned as an agent of European enlightenment.

The narrative begins aboard a cruising yawl called *The Nellie*. A first narrator introduces the scene, explaining that he is sitting aboard the boat, anchored in the Thames estuary waiting for the tide to turn, with four other men: the Director of Companies, who is their host, a lawyer, an accountant and Marlow, who is a seaman. After a short preamble by this unnamed character, Marlow takes over the narrative, as he does similarly in *Lord Jim* (1900), the novel that Conrad interrupted to write *Heart of Darkness*. To pass the time as they wait for the tide, Marlow reminisces about his experience in Africa, which is loosely based on Conrad's own time in the Congo in 1890.

At the start of his story, Marlow, through the help of his aunt, secures the command of a steamboat to travel up the Congo, with which Marlow has long been fascinated; in a similar way, Marlow will become fascinated by the figure of Kurtz. Before he sets off, however, Marlow goes to Léopold's Belgium, to the Brussels headquarters of the company for whom he will be working. The city appears replete with inauspicious omens and Marlow is also disturbed by the strange behaviour of the people he meets there. They view him, by contrast, as an 'emissary of light' travelling into 'the dark continent' as part of Europe's civilising mission. At the offices, Marlow sees a map on which the interests of the various European powers are marked out in colours. Marlow remarks approvingly on the amount of red, the colour of British colonies, where he thinks some 'good' is being done.

On his journey to Africa, Marlow's apprehensions about the colonial enterprise increase. When he reaches the continent, he travels first to the Outer Station, where he is appalled by the inefficiency and rapacity of the colonialists. The Africans are employed in useless laborious tasks, from which they may drop exhausted and be left to die. In contrast to this degradation, the company's chief accountant walks around immaculately dressed and oblivious to the chaos of his surroundings. Marlow finds the order in which the man keeps his books incongruous and absurd in such circumstances.

Marlow's next stop is the Central Station, where he learns that the manager, tired of waiting for him, had already attempted to make the journey to the Inner Station to find Kurtz. In this he had failed, tearing the bottom off the steamer earmarked for Marlow, causing it to sink. In order to repair the boat, Marlow has to send to the Outer Station for rivets, which take two months to arrive. In the meantime, his curiosity about Kurtz increases, though the stories he hears now seem to be less informed by admiration than by fear and anxiety. The manager's uncle, with a group of explorers, arrives at the Central Station. They talk of the wealth that can be squeezed out of Africa. Marlow also overhears the manager and his uncle suggest that they should delay the journey to the Inner Station and that Kurtz should be left to die there as he is already very ill.

Eventually, Marlow sets off for the Inner Station after a three-month delay. He travels with the manager and a small band of pilgrims on a journey that takes an additional two months. In this time, Marlow becomes increasingly preoccupied with Kurtz, a man he always imagines in terms of his voice: his powers of eloquence, persuasion and rhetoric. Marlow feels drawn to the African 'wilderness' too, and it is only his sense of having a job to do, of being occupied, that keeps him from going ashore. At one stage, the boat is attacked from the banks and the African helmsman, who Marlow believes to have been Westernized to the point of being spoiled and without restraint, is killed. The helmsman contrasts with the other Africans on the boat, who Marlow believes to be cannibals and who show great self-restraint, he thinks, by not turning to human flesh when there is little food. Marlow concludes that European civilization has made Westerners flabby and loose in their mission and their morals: they are protected by the butcher and the police, who do their dirty work for them, such that when those checks are removed, colonialists 'go at it blind'.

This is epitomized by Kurtz, who Marlow believes to be the pinnacle of Western culture and civilization, but who proves to be cruel, monomaniacal and savage. The first intimation of this occurs when Marlow realizes that the poles outside Kurtz's house have human heads stuck on them. While he is still onboard the steamer, and the others have disembarked, Marlow meets a young Russian dressed as a harlequin. The man has come aboard to tell Marlow of his unbounded admiration for Kurtz, who has 'expanded [the harlequin's] mind' with his ideas. The harlequin also confesses that it was Kurtz who ordered the steamer to be fired upon earlier.

Kurtz is brought from his house to the shore, very ill and drawn. He is accompanied by many Africans, including a magnificent, gesticulating woman, who is described as his 'mistress'. Kurtz is carried aboard, and Marlow, who is impressed by his voice if not his views, feels some sympathy for him in light of the knowledge of the manager's comments.

That night, Marlow finds that Kurtz has crawled ashore, and goes after him. Marlow manages to bring Kurtz back, but at great cost to himself. Kurtz expatiates on his plans and his power, seducing Marlow with his grand schemes. Kurtz appears unable to distinguish the difference between his ideas and his actions, illustrated by a report he once wrote on the 'Suppression of Savage Customs' over which he has now scrawled 'Exterminate all the brutes'. At his death he calls out 'the horror! the horror!' suggesting he has had some insight or revelation.

Marlow returns to Belgium, despite suffering from an almost fatal fever. He now feels that the people he meets in Brussels are totally ignorant of the conditions of their colonies, and he likens the city to a 'whited sepulchre'. After meeting with several of Kurtz's friends and relations, he visits Kurtz's fiancée, who is known as 'the Intended'. She is a figure about whom Marlow has heard a great deal from Kurtz, and of whom he saw a painting in oils at the Outer Station, showing her as blindfolded and carrying a torch – an ineffective cross between Liberty and Justice. In the room where they meet, the darkness seems to encroach as evening falls, and Marlow notices that the light appears to settle only upon the Intended's pale forehead above her black dress. He is annoyed by her continued faith in Kurtz, and her belief that he was a good man right up to his death. But Marlow is unable to disabuse her and, in fact, reinforces her delusion by falsely saying that Kurtz's last words were her name.

Marlow concludes that the colonialists are themselves tainted by the 'darkness' of their own enterprise, and that the 'light' from the 'sacred flame' of European learning is bright enough to blind its possessor. This is despite the imperial 'idea at the back of it', that civilization is a blessing for all people who are subjected to it. In a way that has been considered racist, Marlow's journey is portrayed as one of travelling back through time as much as it is one along a river, and his first thought is that his most distant kin are of the same blood as he, and therefore he will find himself behaving like a 'savage' if he succumbs to the influence of 'primitive' Africa. All that the colonialists can produce to shield them from this atavism or reversion is their 'civilization', which Marlow and the man he travels to meet, Kurtz, take with them in the form of culture and oratory to envelop the darkness, proclaiming the coming of Europe to Africa like John the Baptist's voice in the wilderness announcing the advent of Christ. However, the novella is itself a disrobing of the European representative Kurtz's 'magnificent eloquence' which leaves him naked in the 'darkness', bereft of a rhetoric which has nothing underneath, revealing him to be a 'hollow' man. Marlow's own downfall following his involvement in the colonial project is to tell a lie, the thing he hates most in the world, to Kurtz's 'Intended'.

As Marlow's tale ends, the first narrator returns and appears to be as affected by Marlow's story as Marlow was by his experience of Kurtz. The opening of the story focuses on the Thames as the point of embarkation of England's great explorers, and on London as the greatest city on earth. The ending has the narrator adopting Marlow's terminology and envisaging the Thames as a river flowing 'into the heart of immense darkness'.

There are several contemporary historical lenses through which the narrative can be viewed, but the novella appears to model itself partly on Henry Stanley's famous quest for David Livingstone. Marlow, like Stanley, is travelling through Africa to find 'the great man'. A reader in 1899 would see the story as a journey into the depths of a continent to find the solitary white soul at the centre. By 1871, when Stanley went to find him in East Africa, Livingstone was famous throughout the Western world, but he had been out of contact for five years. He had decided in 1866 to devote his life to preaching against the slave trade, and was now an icon of the civilizing mission. Stanley's expedition to find him in 1871 was funded by an American newspaper and was perceived, even at the time, as a publicity stunt. The famous meeting was a coup for the press, a staged encounter of two white men in the jungle. Livingstone died two years later, in 1873, and it was then that the cult surrounding him as an individual took off. By the time Conrad was writing, Livingstone was almost a martyr. But this was not the only such encounter, and it was in many ways Stanley who was the key figure. While Livingstone was a missionary and a power for intended good, like Kurtz when he set out for Africa, Stanley used coercion and violence. In terms of his attitudes towards Africans, Stanley was more like the Kurtz Marlow encounters at the Inner Station. After Livingstone's death, Stanley became employed by King Léopold, and he was sent to establish a colony in the Congo region, founding the city of Léopoldville (now Kinshasa). It was Stanley who established the Congo Free State, as it was called between 1879 and 1885. It was 'Free' in so much as Léopold owned it independently of the French, who possessed the rest of the Congo. Stanley finally retired in 1890 (the year that Conrad made his own journey up the Congo) and became a Member of Parliament.

Heart of Darkness seems to inaugurate modernism because of its deep sense of doubt, epistemological and existential. Language is no longer a mirror, but a distorting lens, and 'progress' is unmasked as hollow rhetoric. The narrative and narration exemplify the seven characteristics outlined by Raymond Williams in 'When was Modernism?' (Williams: 31–5). First, there is the alignment with Freud's emphasis on the unconscious: Marlow's journey is one into his own psychological makeup. There is also a radical disbelief in the process of representation, as Marlow worries both if he might be dreaming and whether anyone will understand his traumatic experience: words fail him as the light fails on *The Nellie* while he recites his story. In Conrad's story, there is additionally the problematic status of the authority of the narrator, whose unreliability is plain even to himself. Williams also points to the artist as anticommercial radical, and while this does not really fit Conrad's history, it implies the stance Marlow takes against capitalist greed and colonial exploitation. Williams identifies the importance of the 'new metropolitan cities': the 'City of Strangers' and 'transnational capitals', which is evident in Marlow's portrayal of Brussels, but also the sheer internationalism of the story, starting in London and travelling to Belgium, then Africa. Then there is the modernist facet of art made by the émigré or exile: Conrad is the archetypal traveller and migrant of modernism, following a life at sea with becoming a naturalized British citizen. Lastly, Williams identifies the artificial status of language as a key modernist element, and this is perhaps the most intriguing aspect to Conrad's story, which from its start ponders the ability of language to represent the world: 'to [Marlow] the meaning of an episode was not inside like a kernel but outside, enveloping the tale which brought it out only as a glow brings out a haze, in the likeness of one of those misty halos that sometimes are made visible by the spectral illumination of moonshine' (Conrad 1973: 30).

The beneficence of the triumphant technological advance of the West also begins to be questioned in Conrad's work. In 'Geography and Some Explorers', collected in *Last Essays* (1926), Conrad wrote about how he felt when he arrived at Stanley Falls: 'Yes, this was the very spot. But there was no shadowy friend to stand by my side in the night of the enormous wilderness, no great haunting memory, but only the unholy recollection of a prosaic newspaper "stunt" and the distasteful knowledge of the vilest scramble for loot that ever disfigured the history of human conscience...' (Conrad 1944: 113).

LORD JIM: A TALE (1900)

Lord Jim (1900) was Conrad's fourth novel, after *Almayer's Folly* (1895), *An Outcast of the Islands* (1896), and *The Nigger of the 'Narcissus'* (1897), a shorter work. Conrad had intended next to produce *The Rescue*, the final part of the Malayan trilogy begun by his first two novels, but, despite having received advances, he struggled with the material, and it was not published until 1920. Meeting Ford Madox Ford in 1898 appears to have been a turning point for Conrad, who then, materially and artistically supported by his new friend, set out on the major creative phase of his life, beginning with the stories narrated by Marlow and lasting up to the First World War.

Serialized in *Blackwood's Magazine*, like *Heart of Darkness*, *Lord Jim* is also introduced by a framing narrator who sketches the novel's protagonist in broad-brush terms before Captain Charles Marlow takes over in Chapter 5. The two men, along with others, are passing the time on a veranda after dinner by telling yarns.

As his 'yarn' is unwoven we learn that Marlow has been a close friend of the eponymous hero from the time of Jim's notorious 'jump' from an overcrowded pilgrim ship called the *Patna* when it encountered difficulties after hitting something in the water. Conrad's tale of the *Patna* is based on the true story of the S.S. *Jeddah*, a steamer bound from Singapore to Jeddah, which in August 1880 was caught in bad weather off the east coast of Africa, abandoned by its captain and engineers, and reported foundered, but in fact towed safely to Aden. Jim's punishment for his desertion of the *Patna* is to have his certificate cancelled. As they leave the court, Jim meets Marlow when a companion of the latter calls a wretched dog they see a 'cur', and Jim, overhearing the remark from ahead, thinks the speaker is Marlow and the object of the comment himself. Jim's reaction to this misunderstanding is the point at which Marlow becomes fascinated by him and seeks to befriend him.

Jim takes up various employments and 'wanders' over the 3,000 miles of the Eastern seaboard trying to escape his past (there are many comparisons to Christ and to the Wandering Jew). Marlow says: 'For instance, in Bankok [sic], where he found employment with Yucker Brothers, charterers and teak merchants, it was almost pathetic to see him go about in sunshine hugging his secret, which was known to the very up-country logs on the river' (Chapter 19). Soon after this, following Jim's involvement in a bar fight, Marlow decides to go and see a 'wealthy and respected merchant' called Stein. It is Stein who fixes Jim up with the project that will occupy the rest of the book, but he also utters the most enigmatic, but perhaps for Conrad most important, speech in the novel:

> 'We want in so many ways to be', he began again. 'This magnificent butterfly finds a little heap of dirt and sits still on it; but man will never on his heap of mud keep still. He want to be so, and again he want to be so ... ' He moved his hand up, then down ... 'He wants to be a saint, and he wants to be a devil – and every time he shuts his eyes he sees himself as a very fine fellow – so fine as he can never be ... In a dream ... ' [...] 'And because you not always can keep your eyes shut there comes the real trouble – the heart pain – the world pain. I tell you, my friend, it is not good for you to find you cannot make your dream come true, for the reason that you not strong enough are, or not clever enough. *Ja!* ... And all the time you are such a fine fellow too! *Wie? Was? Gott im Himmel!* How can that be? Ha! ha! ha!' [...] 'Yes! Very funny this terrible thing is. A man that is born falls into a dream like a man falls into the sea. If he tries to climb out into the air as inexperienced people endeavour to do, he drowns – *nicht wahr?* ... No! I tell you! The way is to the destructive element submit yourself, and with the exertions of your hands and feet in the water make the deep, deep sea keep you up.' (Chapter 20)

Like much of the tenor of *Heart of Darkness*, Stein's speech questions how much individuals can know themselves and how unified are a person's mind, desires and thoughts. Published in the same year as Freud's *Interpretations of Dreams*, Conrad's novel reflects a world of split personalities, unconscious drives and fragmented dreams.

Stein asks Jim to replace the agent, a Portuguese man called Cornelius, at his trading post in Patusan (a fictional country situated by Conrad in the Malay Archipelago). Both the district of Patusan and the country-born Malays are exploited by Rajah Allang, one of the Sultan's uncles and the royal governor of the local river. Jim is sent with a letter of dismissal for Cornelius and a silver ring. The ring is to serve as an introduction to Doramin, a local chief and an old friend of Stein's. On arrival however, Jim is imprisoned in the stockade for three days and has to make two desperate 'leaps', the first over some stakes and the second over a muddy creek, in order to escape and find Doramin. Doramin, the elected head of the Bugis immigrants from nearby Celebes, is involved in numerous quarrels with the Rajah, who wants a monopoly on trade. Jim forms a firm friendship with Doramin's son, Dain Waris: 'one of those strange, profound rare friendships between brown and white, in which the very difference of race seems to draw two human beings closer by some mystic element of sympathy' (Chapter 26). Jim persuades Doramin to attack the bandit Sherif Ali's camp, which they successfully capture, forcing Ali to flee the country (Ali, with Cornelius's help, later sends four men to try to kill Jim). Jim appoints the new headman and so becomes powerful in the district. He also has the help of a man called Tamb' Itam ('black messenger'), who is devoted to him, and forms a relationship with Jewel, the daughter of Cornelius's wife.

Marlow's narrative pauses, and the first narrator returns briefly to explain that the conclusion of the story was sent by Marlow two years later to one of the listeners on the veranda. Marlow has learned what became of Jim from two sources: first, he met Tamb' Itam at Stein's, and second, he came across a dying man called Gentleman Brown in Bangkok. Brown, a 'latter-day buccaneer', turned up in Patusan requiring provisions while Jim was away in the interior. Dain Waris tried to repulse Brown's ship, but when talks opened up between the two parties Cornelius acted as an interpreter and tried to persuade Brown that he should usurp 'Tuan Jim': 'Lord Jim'. When Jim returned, Brown took an instant dislike to the young, self-righteous man, but his own speech, asking for sympathy and understanding, struck a chord in Jim, who decided to let Brown go unhindered. Dain Waris was not sure this was wise, and set up a camp on the island to see that 'the white robbers' sailed away without incident. However, Brown landed his men by a narrow channel at the back of the island

and maliciously ambushed the Bugis camp. Dain Waris was shot in the forehead and killed before Brown made off.

A mortified Jim accepted full responsibility for this disaster and went to face Doramin, Dain Waris's father. The old man took up the pistols Stein gave him in exchange for the ring Jim returned to him as his introduction to Doramin, and, rising to his feet, causing the ring to fall from his lap and roll to Jim's feet, shot his son's friend through the chest.

Following Stein's speech quoted above, it can be argued that the book asks the reader to contemplate the difficulties of deciding between an honourable course of action which appears risky and a practical course which seems dishonourable. Most critics debate the sympathies that Marlow and Conrad have with Jim, attempting to determine the degree to which he should be viewed harshly or leniently. It is a critical commonplace to argue that the book falls too obviously into two halves, with the second Patusan section weaker than the first *Patna* chapters. Conrad had intended to leave the book after the *Patna* episode, but evidently felt there was scope to develop the story into a symmetrical narrative of a fall from professional and personal honour followed by an opportunity for redemption. From a modernist perspective, the novel is chiefly notable for its use of impressionism and symbolism: it is one of the first novels to eschew direct linear narrative for atmospheric and enigmatic narration, placing it in a style somewhere between that of Conrad's literary role model, Flaubert, and high modernism. The tone is almost unremittingly bleak, and the outlook pessimistic. The novel's reputation is perhaps not as high in the twenty-first century as it was 30 or more years ago, but it is a valuable text. This is both in terms of Conrad's view of imperialism and as a comparison to the presentation of Marlow in *Heart of Darkness*, together with Marlow's attitudes towards Kurtz, who is in some ways a negative image of the equally egotistical Jim. Marlow is the narrator of two more of Conrad's works: 'Youth' (1902) and *Chance* (1913).

NOSTROMO: A TALE OF THE SEABOARD (1904)

Conrad's next novel, *Nostromo*, is set on the north coast of South America, in the fictional country of Costaguana. The story line concerns the revolutionary and evolutionary phases in the birth of a Latin republic, from the injection of British and U.S. capital into the conflict-ridden province to its emergence as a new state. At the centre of the political strand of the story is a revolution. Don Vincente Ribiera, who oversees a benign five-year dictatorship, is the first civilian Chief of the State ever known in Costaguana. He is described by the narrator as 'a man of culture and of unblemished character, invested with a mandate of reform by the best elements of the State'. He is overthrown by former Minister of War and rural hero General Montero, who evokes 'the exaggeration of a cruel caricature, the fatuity of solemn masquerading, the atrocious grotesqueness of some military idol of Aztec conception and European bedecking, awaiting the homage of worshippers' (Chapter 8).

Epic in scale, with in excess of 70 notable characters, *Nostromo* is a complex modernist novel that does not unfold in any kind of linear fashion; readers are sometimes at a loss as to when and where events are taking place, and so have to rely on 'delayed decoding': piecing together parts of the narrative at a later stage. First published as a serial in *T. P.'s Weekly*, the book is divided into three parts: 'The Silver of the Mine', 'The Isabels', and 'The Lighthouse'. As is found in several of Conrad's works, the overarching narrator appears to be an all-knowing third-person commentator, and yet is evidently also an observer in the fictional universe of the story who slips very occasionally into the first person: 'Those of us whom business or curiosity took to Sulaco in these years before the first advent of the railway' (Chapter 8). Conrad's principal narrator thus appears to be composing a 'tale' of Costaguana, and particularly Sulaco, a city in the Occidental Province of the Republic, from a number of sources, reports and perspectives, yet is also granted privileged knowledge of information and events that only an omniscient perspective could provide.

Part 1 moves back in time from the present of the novel, which is generally taken to be 1890, and critics have noted that only a tenth of Part 1 actually takes place in the present of the narrative. After a panoramic overview of Sulaco and its region, spiced with local folklore and intimations of its history of adventure and treasure seeking, the book introduces Captain Mitchell, the elderly superintendent of the Oceanic Steam Navigation Company, who will narrate some of the story. The reader learns of the coming of President Ribiera, the benign dictator of Costaguana, and also his rescue, when the latest uprising begins, instigated by Mitchell and his Capataz de Cargadores, Gian' Battista Fidanza, who is nicknamed Nostromo ('our man'). Nostromo lives with the Viola family: Giorgio Viola, keeper

of the Casa Viola and veteran of Garibaldi's army; Tersea, his neur-
otic, sickly wife; Linda, their idealistic elder daughter; and Giselle,
their sensual younger daughter. Both daughters are in love with
Nostromo. After introducing these characters, the narrative moves
back 18 months to the time of Ribiera's opening of the National
Central Railway. We are introduced to Sir John, chairman of the railway board; Charles Gould, the manager of the San Tomé silver mine
near Sulaco; and his wife Emilia, the moral centre of the novel. We
also learn of the history of General Montero, who will lead the revolution against Ribiera.

In Part 2, through the introduction of a patriotic and idealistic
statesman, Don José Avellanos, author of a history of the country
called 'Fifty Years of Misrule', the reader is given an overview of the
history of Costaguana and Sulaco, and in particular the figures of
the former dictator Guzman Bento, the Montero family, President
Ribiera, and General Barrios, the Commander of the Occidental
military district. The other major character introduced in this run up
to the revolution's climax and Ribiera's escape, mentioned at the
start of the novel, is Martin Decoud, a young Creole journalist newly
returned from Paris with the vision of a separate Occidental Republic. Mrs Gould gives her support to Decoud's plans for an independent Sulaco, and Decoud reveals the full story of Ribiera's rescue by
Nostromo, with whom he then meets. Decoud and Nostromo set off
on in a lighter to one of the barren islands in the harbour entrance
known as the three Isabels to save from the revolutionaries a cargo
of silver brought down from the mine. However, their boat is struck
by a steamer carrying Monterist troops, and it begins to sink. Nostromo steers the lighter to the Great Isabel island and leaves Decoud
there with the silver they have buried while he, strong enough to
swim the distance, escapes back to the mainland.

Part 3 is considerably longer than the previous two. The steamer
that struck the lighter turns out to have been carrying the traitorous
General Sotillo, one of the leaders of the revolution hurrying to
Sulaco for personal gain. The Europeans in Sulaco scatter as the city
is taken over by two officials who throw their lot in with the Monte-
ros. Pedrito Montero, the General's brother, enters Sulaco and sends
a messenger to demand the obedience of the mine. Don Pépé, its
overseer, who is under orders to blow up San Tomé if the revolutionaries take it, refuses to hand over control. Gould also refuses, and is
taken prisoner before Nostromo is persuaded to ride off and bring

back General Barrios from Cayta. Don Pépé attacks Sulaco at Land Gate and rescues Gould. Meanwhile, Nostromo arrives back with Barrios, who attacks Sotillo's ship and then storms Sulaco from Harbour Gate. The city is saved, and two weeks later a new constitution is announced for an independent Sulaco. A Civil War ensues.

Two hundred pages after telling of his abandonment, the narrator now explains Decoud's lonely suicide, drowning himself by using some of the silver as weights, after ten days isolated on the island. When Nostromo finds that Decoud is gone and that the silver, which everyone else thinks has sunk in the harbour, is abandoned on the island, he resolves to get rich slowly by returning occasionally for a few ingots.

The last three chapters go forward in time, covering the period up to 1900. The Civil War ends in 1891 and Montero is assassinated. The province becomes the Occidental Republic and is open to the speculations and investments of financiers and entrepreneurs. Gould, who took a place at the centre of the party for freedom and justice, becomes increasingly estranged from Emilia and dehumanized by his preoccupation with the silver mine and 'material interests'. In 1898, a lighthouse is built on the island of Great Isabel, and the Violas become its keepers. Two years later, there is labour unrest, and some politicians in Sulaco are planning to annex Costaguana to Sulaco. Nostromo, who is still considered the epitome of integrity, continues to take silver from the stashed horde on the Great Isabel. He is now engaged to Linda, but in love with Giselle. The novel ends when he visits the island on one occasion and is mistaken for Ramirez the Vagabond, a despised suitor of Giselle, by the elderly Viola, who shoots him. On his deathbed, Nostromo attempts to confess to Mrs Gould, but she will not listen, and his reputation remains spotless.

The positive and negative outlooks on the events of the novel are expressed respectively by two characters: Captain Mitchell and Dr Monygham. After the establishment of the new Republic, Mitchell believes that, with a democratic government and civil institutions, investors and property owners can look forward to security while the people can live in peace. For Monygham, however, 'material interests', which are inhuman, will provide no peace or rest: 'the time approaches when all that the Gould Concession stands for shall weigh as heavily upon the people as the barbarism, cruelty and misrule of a few years back.' The silver represents both of these positions, because it is itself valuable and incorruptible but corrupts and devalues the people who come into contact with it. These two perspectives are contrasted in the novel, inviting the reader to choose which they favour, like the choices outlined above for *Heart of Darkness* and *Lord Jim*, where idealism and pragmatism are opposed, flawed alternatives.

Cedric Watts identifies the major factor that differentiates *Nostromo* from previous fiction as an extreme mobility of viewpoint: the juxtaposition of different time periods, the alternation between close and distant perspectives on scenes, the shifts between narrators and narrative focalizers, and the multiplicity of similarities, analogies, and pointed contrasts between characters. In terms of subject matter, the novel seems to express Conrad's profound political pessimism. He wrote, in an essay on Anatole France: 'Political institutions, whether contrived by the wisdom of the few or the ignorance of the many, are incapable of securing the happiness of mankind.' (Conrad 2002: 32). *Nostromo* also rests on the incompatibility of ideals and 'material interests', which can be variously understood as individual financial speculation or the forces of imperialism. The silver in the story, mentioned every time Nostromo himself appears in the narrative, is the main subject and symbol of the novel: it is the reason all the characters are drawn to Costaguana and the cause of their inevitable corruption, tainting revolutionary, imperialist, liberal, civilian and soldier alike. The novel's appeal, for many current critics, lies in its complex depiction of colonial relations and imperial exploitation. Yet its complexity, which has gained it a reputation as a novel you can only read properly if you have read it before, typifies the difficulty that is associated with modernism.

THE SECRET AGENT: A SIMPLE TALE (1907)

As he also does for his later novel *Under Western Eyes* (1911), Conrad draws on his understanding of different ideologies, imperial ambitions and revolutionary activity in the decades around the turn of the century for *The Secret Agent*. The novel moves between several groups of characters, the most prominent of which is the band of backstreet anarchists and revolutionaries who congregate around Mr Verloc, a seedy shop owner, but also a spy. Set around 1895 in London and inspired by a real incident of 1894, the plot builds towards an attempt by Verloc to bomb the Greenwich Observatory – the place from which time has been calibrated around the world since an agreement reached by scientists in Rome in 1883 and then endorsed by a meeting of official government delegates at Washington in 1884. This agreement followed on from the use of British charts by a large proportion of the world's shipping, coupled with the adoption in North America of time zones based on the Greenwich meridian. The chosen site for the bombing is therefore of great significance, in terms of science, empire and international fame. The book also has a context of Anglo-Russian imperial tensions in the 1890s and Conrad's understanding of the failed Russian revolution of 1905.

The Secret Agent is most easily seen as a story of anarchists in late nineteenth-century London, when most political activists in England were refugees keen to maintain the authorities' tolerance. Conrad's novel concerns the attempt of other European powers to provoke an outrage that will change the British government's permissive attitude. With little reason to worry over assassination attempts and terrorist activity, late Victorian society went without immigration controls until the turn of the century.

Unlike *Nostromo*, *The Secret Agent* is an easy narrative for the reader to follow. Unusually for Conrad, it also has a comparatively small cast of characters, maintains a consistent narrational persona and perspective, contains few references to imperialism, and is not set aboard ship or abroad. The book was first published in serial form in *Ridgeway's* magazine.

The opening chapters of the novel introduce the Verloc family. Adolf Verloc is a lazy *agent provocateur* who is 'constitutionally averse from every superfluous exertion'. He is described as 'Undemonstrative and burly in a fat-pig style'. He runs a small Soho stationer's, which mainly sells pornography. Verloc's wife, Winnie, has married him to provide for her ailing mother and slow-witted brother, Stevie, whom she adores and watches over with 'maternal vigilance'. By contrast, Verloc extends 'as much recognition to Stevie as a man not particularly fond of animals may give to his wife's beloved cat' (Chapter 2).

More attention is given to the group of anarchists who meet at Verloc's house. These include an idealistic and harmless ex-convict Michaelis who, after 15 years in prison, revels in the patronage of a society woman, Lady Mabel, and a malevolent, decrepit 'terrorist' called Karl Yundt, who talks much and does little. Yundt is dependent upon an elderly woman, while the last member of the group, Comrade

Ossipon, seduces young women who have money. Ossipon thus com-
pletes the impression of men supported, financially and emotionally,
by women they can deceive into thinking they are romantic figures.

The story's main plot is set in motion when Verloc is sent for by
one of the foreign embassies, seemingly the Russian, for which he
secretly works. Once there he finds that the first secretary at the
embassy, Mr Vladimir, wishes to influence a meeting of European
representatives in Milan on the issue of political activism: ' "England
lags. This country is absurd with its sentimental regard for individual
liberty"' (Chapter 2). Vladimir therefore requests from Verloc an
'outrage', such as the bombing of the Observatory.

The Greenwich bombing is actually attempted about a month
after Verloc visits Mr Vladimir. Ossipon, talking to a specialist on
explosives, called the Professor, finds out that Verloc had recently
procured a bomb from him. The reader will not know for 100 pages,
half of the book, that Stevie has been killed by the explosion and not
Verloc, as most of the characters assume. The deformed Professor,
who dreams of making the perfect detonator, advises Ossipon, a former medical student whose nickname is the Doctor, to latch on to
Winnie.

The Secret Agent also portrays the authorities investigating the
bombing. The most important is Chief Inspector Heat, who reports
to the assistant commissioner of police, and, having recently returned
from colonial service, believes in 'unconventional' methods. For personal reasons, Heat is convinced that Michaelis is behind the bungled
bomb attempt, but the assistant commissioner is a friend of Lady
Mabel's, and so insists on further investigations, which he will partly
undertake himself. Heat shows the assistant commissioner the scrap
of material found at the scene of the explosion: a charred label which
Winnie had sewn into Stevie's clothing with the address 32 Brett
Street. The assistant commissioner then visits the home secretary,
Sir Ethelred, and advises him of his plan to force Verloc to reveal the
perpetrators.

The narrative then makes a characteristic Conradian leap back in
time to before the bombing. Winnie's mother has moved out to an
almshouse so that Stevie will be better cared for when Verloc's respon-
sibilities are reduced. In line with this, Verloc duly takes Stevie for a
holiday with Michaelis outside of the city, though he proves to have
other plans for the boy. On the evening of the day of the 'outrage',
Verloc returns to the shop and receives two visitors. The first is the

assistant commissioner and the second, later that evening, is Chief Inspector Heat. As Verloc talks to Heat, Winnie overhears some of their conversation and realizes Stevie has been killed. She learns that Verloc, uprooting Stevie from his holiday with Michaelis, took him to Greenwich along with the Professor's homemade explosive device, and then sent Stevie ahead to blow up the Observatory; but Stevie tripped and fell to the ground clutching what he did not even know was a bomb.

Distressed by Stevie's death, Winnie kills Verloc by stabbing him and flees with their savings. Outside she meets Ossipon, who is delighted by her attentions until he realizes that she has murdered her husband. Hiding his horror, he encourages her to give him her money and let him take her to Paris. However, Ossipon jumps out of the train as it leaves Waterloo. Shortly after, he reads a newspaper report of a woman who leapt from a steamer into the Channel and realizes that Winnie has drowned herself at sea. He is distraught, but the Professor is stoical, reasserting his faith in destruction. The closing scene of the novel has the Professor walking off into the darkness of London's streets, still clutching the detonator that he will fire if the police attempt to arrest him.

The Secret Agent is one of Conrad's most chilling works, and it is also unusual in his canon in being set in England. Conrad creates an eerily Dickensian seedy London and the narration also uses Dickens's metonymic techniques, particularly synecdoche and reification. It is as bleak as Conrad's other works and is notable in revealing every character to be misled. No one really knows what is going on – most are deceived by Verloc, but he himself is ignorant of the label Winnie has sewn into Stevie's coat. The two admirable characters, Winnie and Stevie, both care for others and cannot bear suffering. Stevie's simple-minded desire for everyone to be happy and for there to be no pain appears to be a reflection, if not a mockery, of the anarchists' ambitions. That he is the unwitting bomber and the innocent victim is one of the ironies of the plot. It is also indicative of Conrad's pessimism that the most caring character, Winnie, becomes the one murderer in the novel and then kills herself, too. Critics have suggested that the book could be considered a novel about the pointlessness of all endeavour and all aspiration, but it has a precise setting in the context of the birth of modern terrorism. It is also somewhat sceptical in its portrayal of those who try to improve life, from either side of the law. The police are seen simply as preservers of an unjust *status quo*, as Winnie explains to Stevie: 'They are there so that them as have nothing shouldn't take anything away from them who have' (Chapter 7).

The Secret Agent has been said to be one of the four major English novels that envision the disintegration of society that occurred in 1914, along with H. G. Wells's *Tono-Bungay* (1909), D. H. Lawrence's *Women in Love* (completed near the beginning of the war but not published until 1920), and E. M. Forster's *Howards End* (1910).

THE WINGS OF THE DOVE (1902)

Henry James (1843–1916) was born in New York and tutored privately in America and Europe. He attended Harvard law school but dropped out to study literature and write. He spent the last 40 years of his life in England, becoming a British subject in the year before his death.

James's novels have been divided into periods, from his early works, such as *The American* (1877) and *The Europeans* (1878), through to the complex late novels considered here: *The Wings of the Dove* (1902), *The Ambassadors* (1903), and *The Golden Bowl* (1904), which are dense and closely written texts that have been likened to impressionist painting.

James's contribution to the theory of the novel is as important as his fiction. In particular, his 1884 essay 'The Art of Fiction' and his prefaces to the New York editions (1907–9) of his complete works constitute the fullest articulations of a novelist's approach to writing. One of the most important aspects to his novelistic approach was his emphasis on focalization: on detailing the perspective of a character as an embodied narrator. The importance of the subjectivity of experience was one of the legacies James gave to later writers, along with the minute attention to expression in long, intricate sentences that accrete layers of meaning around an initial thought. James emphasized a scrupulous 'realism' as his aim, but in this he took the novel towards modernist styles of writing, emphasizing interiority and a complete attention to precise expression.

James's late novels are explorations in thought, rather than action, and the plots become thinner as the accent on consciousness grows. In *The Wings of the Dove*, James seeks to show Kate Croy in her human complexity, which means that her deeds are much more richly understood by the reader through an appreciation of how her actions are conceived in her mind. An external depiction of Kate might force her to appear simply manipulative and callous, but James insinuates considerable doubt in the reader's mind by the multisided portrayal of her motivation.

Set mostly in London, the story follows the descent of Kate, hopelessly dependent on a corrupt and dishonourable father, into deception and emotional manipulation after her social adoption by a wealthy aunt, Mrs Lowder. Kate is in love with and engaged to a poor journalist, Densher, who she has little chance of marrying, because they have no money. Following an introduction by her aunt to Milly Theale, Kate comes to see a possibility of happiness. Milly is an attractive American heiress who has met and fallen in love with Densher while he was on a trip to the States. However, after a visit to the doctor, Kate discovers that Milly may also be terminally ill. A plan hatches slowly in Kate's mind and she confesses it to Densher at a party Milly throws in Venice, where she has gone to consider how she is affected by her illness. When he realizes Kate proposes he should marry Milly in order to inherit her wealth when she dies, Densher insists that they consummate their love.

Densher remains in Venice to court Milly, while Kate returns to London. Their plot is found out, however, when an old suitor of Kate's reveals the plan to Milly, whose health and spirits quickly deteriorate. Densher sees her one last time before Milly dies, then he leaves for London. Surprisingly, Milly bequeaths Densher a considerable legacy in her will.

Densher is conscience-stricken and tells Kate that he cannot accept the money and marry her. In fact, he believes he should renounce the inheritance, but offers to give the money to Kate if she would prefer the wealth to his love and continued poverty. Kate is more concerned that Densher is now in love with the memory of Milly, even though he offers to marry her 'as we were'. Her reply closes the book: 'We shall never be again as we were!'

The style of the novel exemplifies James's belief in showing rather than telling the reader the situations and motivations of characters. As he remarks in the New York edition preface:

> The building-up of Kate Croy's consciousness to the capacity for the load little by little to be laid on it was, by way of example, to have been a matter of as many hundred close-packed bricks as there are actually poor dozens. The image of her so compromised and

compromising father was all effectively to have pervaded her life, was in a certain particular way to have tampered with her spring; by which I mean that the shame and the irritation and the depression, the general poisonous influence of him, were to have been SHOWN, with a truth beyond the compass even of one's most emphasised 'word of honour' for it, to do these things. (James 2005: 11)

The practice of showing rather than telling in itself introduces layers of ambiguity, because the reader is forced to draw conclusions without the guiding hand of the author's commentary. This brings the art of fiction closer to life for James because, as in life, there is no final arbiter of meaning, even though all the abundance of life is set before us to make sense of. Building on the examples of Hawthorne, Eliot, Turgenev, Flaubert and others, James above all asserted that the novel was an art form, on a par with poetry and painting. To demonstrate this, the serious novelist had to pay close attention to life and take scrupulous care with its rendition in fiction.

THE AMBASSADORS (1903)

Modernism is in part characterized by its concern with the depiction of the mind, and in this James is a seminal influence. Known as 'The Master' to younger writers because of his dedication to technique, James was most interested in the mental awareness of his characters, evident in the detailed portrayal of their thoughts. The representation of consciousness, increasingly seen in terms of fluidity, was a principal aim of James's later works, which sought to examine the complexity of the mind, patterns of feeling, moral awareness, and psychological insight.

James thought *The Ambassadors* his finest novel. Its plot is a familiar one in fiction and centres on an envoy, Lambert Strether, sent to prise back a young American, Chad, sequestered in Europe. However, hailing from a New England background, Strether becomes enamoured of the old world, and the inquiry into how and why he does not fulfil his role as an ambassador is the core of the novel's interest.

The 55-year-old Strether is sent to Paris by his fiancée, Mrs Newsome, to find and return her son, who is enwrapped in a relationship with the alluring Marie de Vionnet. It is assumed she is corrupting the young American. His task is set aside as Strether comes to a fuller understanding of the differences between the culture of America and Europe, the limitations of his own life choices and experience, and the benefits of a self-determination that Chad has shown in an attachment of which Strether comes to approve. Strether concludes that it is better to choose your own life and make your own mistakes than simply to follow convention and duty: 'Live all you can; it's a mistake not to', he concludes.

In effect, Lambert Strether becomes far more interested in his own self-knowledge, finer thoughts, and available choices than in his ostensible reason for coming to Europe. Similarly, the focus of the novel is not on external journeys and intrigues, but on internal ones. This encapsulates the deeper reality that modernists sought to render in techniques from Dorothy Richardson's stream of consciousness to Virginia Woolf's 'tunnelling' into the past through characters' memories. The depiction of mental processes was also the characteristic that might be specific to the novel as an art form, and so be used to argue its particularity and its value. James saw the imaginative power of art, familiar in poetry, music and painting, as the necessary transforming force that would take the novel from its social, descriptive representation of reality into a higher realism characterized by aesthetics, psychology and analysis.

Focalizing the narrative through one consciousness took the device of free indirect discourse in James's fiction further than would have been discernible in the nineteenth-century's finest novelists, from Austen to George Eliot. This technique provided narratorial consciousnesses in these late novels who were not omniscient, but who perceived acutely their own thoughts and feelings as well as the society, sensations and individuals around them. The author's presence is therefore felt less clearly by the reader, who at any point reads circumstances through the prism of a character who is nonetheless not a first-person narrator. The reader is guided through the story by characters' perspectives and their understanding determines the reader's apprehension of the story without the conceit of a disembodied, third-person voice commenting on events and characters. The reader also has to see through the characters' limitations to understand events from more than one angle and gain a fuller picture. James's method has been hailed as a revolutionary one, but it won little favour with the general public, who preferred easier reading matter. James's sentences pile clause upon clause in a highly nuanced but dense style that can be off-putting, and which also signals the aesthetic sophistication that will come to be associated with modernism and particularly with writers like Joyce, Woolf, Stein and Richardson.

For James, this is more correctly seen as precision, and he developed an elaborate style of grammar and expression to convey human complexity. In 'The Art of Fiction', he wrote that 'to "render" the simplest surface, to produce the most momentary illusion, is a very complicated business' (James 1965: 62). It is thus that, for James, the drama takes place in the language, where an intense attention to the nuances of human behaviour has to be shown in minute detail, with a distinct focus and clarity.

THE GOLDEN BOWL (1904) AND *THE HOUSE OF MIRTH* (1905)

The title of this late 'major phase' James novel, a quotation from Eccl. 12:.6, illustrates a common approach to naming among modernists: 'the golden bowl be broken ... then shall the dust return to the earth'. It both refers to an actual gift within the story and acts as the book's central metaphor. The story takes place in London and concerns a tight group of four characters: young heiress Maggie Verver, her art collector father Adam, Charlotte Stant, and impoverished Prince Amerigo, an Italian nobleman. Echoing a theme from *The Wings of a Dove*, Charlotte is the poor friend of Maggie and in love with Maggie's fiancé Amerigo. When Charlotte and Amerigo search for a wedding gift for Maggie, they discover a beautiful crystal bowl, which in the end they do not buy because Amerigo thinks it has a tiny, almost imperceptible, but nonetheless significant, flaw. Maggie later buys the selfsame gilded bowl as a gift for her father, who is to take Charlotte's hand in marriage. The defect in this seemingly happy situation is the resumption of their previous love affair by Amerigo and Charlotte, leaving Maggie and her father betrayed. On discovering the deception, by means of the bowl itself, Maggie's reaction is to decide to send her friend away, even at the cost of losing her father, the close relationship with whom both led her to suggest his marriage and resulted in Amerigo and Charlotte spending long periods of time together, prompting their renewed intimacy. Keeping the affair a secret from him, Maggie persuades her father to return to America with Charlotte.

The Golden Bowl is James's final great novel, though several other works were to follow in his last dozen years. The story is again presented through the consciousness of the central characters. Of these, Maggie is the principal focus, and it is her journey from innocence to experience that most engages the reader. Overdependent on her emotional attachment to her father, Maggie is prompted by Charlotte and Amerigo's betrayal to realize the need for her to commit herself to her marriage by creating a distance not just between the adulterous couple, but also between Adam and her.

The novel has a strongly claustrophobic feel, because of the intense concentration on four characters and the perceptions of Maggie and Amerigo in particular. The other major participants in the story are the Assinghams, a couple who comment and conjecture on the central quartet. Another sad story of American moral education in the Old World, *The Golden Bowl* has been praised for its delicate treatment of marriage, but criticized for its slow pace and concentrated analyses of each nuance of feeling. A novel about the imperfections that lie beneath the surface of polite society, it is also about the relationships between the rich and the comparatively poor in turn-of-the-century Europe, and about the American expatriate's sense of being both insider and outsider in Europe. It is also concerned with anti-Semitism: the antique dealer who sells the gilded bowl is a Jew whose wares are rejected by Amerigo for no apparent reason. But above all, it is of course about attention to detail: the supposed blemish in the bowl does not go unremarked, and for James 'Everything counts, nothing is superfluous', as he wrote in the preface to an earlier novel, *Roderick Hudson*.

James's late novels also found a companion piece in the first novel of Edith Wharton, published the year after *The Golden Bowl*. Wharton's *The House of Mirth* is a narrative about reliance on money in the upper classes and the conflicts between an old and new order. With the added attraction of a serious analysis of gender alongside class and social snobbery, Wharton's book looks at the transition stateside from Old New York manners to modern materialism. Its heroine is Lily Bart, a young and beautiful but poor member of the social elite. Echoing a theme prominent in James's late novels, Lily's only security will be to marry into money. Again, there is the sense of a gilded world, whose veneer will be exposed as in *The Golden Bowl* or *Heart of Darkness*. Lily wishes to find a meaningful relationship, but is forced to think only of the social game of courtship. Her world appears genteel and civilized, but is, in fact, quite brutalized and brutalizing. She wishes to act ethically, but finds emotional and material corruption surrounding her. Games of bribery and seduction end badly, such that Lily has to drop out of polite society and find increasingly menial employment. Finally, she dies from a sleeping-drug overdose, her intelligence and morals unvalued by an inhumane social environment. Though not proto-modernist in style, like James's late work, Wharton's novel incorporates a new social voice that transforms the novel of manners into a class-based critique of an immoral money culture whose treatment of women remains deeply uncivilized. An important influence on twentieth-century American literature, like James, Wharton is also a fine exponent of the novel of tribal etiquette and social hypocrisy, whose later masterpiece *The Age of Influence* (1920) was an anthropological dissection of the similarly suffocating rituals of nineteenth-century New York aristocracy.

IRISH THEATRE AND *THE PLAYBOY OF THE WESTERN WORLD* (1907)

Though George Bernard Shaw and Oscar Wilde were Irish dramatists who took to the London stage and London society, Irish theatre was more radically revolutionized than British drama at the turn of the century. W. B. Yeats wished to develop an Irish culture based on traditional and mythological themes, even though his Abbey Theatre thrived by staging the popular comedies preferred by audiences. Yeats's own plays, from *The Shadowy Waters* (1895) up to *The Death of Cuchulain* (1939), developed from an early symbolism to a more abstract, mythological form of presentation, influenced by anti-realist Japanese Noh theatre, which aspires to archetypes of music and dance, rather than dramatic presentation. Much of Yeats's drama, and notably the best-known early plays *Cathleen Ni Houlihan* (1902) and *On Baile's Strand* (1904), was written as part of an attempt to develop both a national mythology and an Irish theatre in Dublin.

Two prominent dramatists associated with the Abbey Theatre were J. M. Synge (1871–1909) and, later, Sean O'Casey (1880–1964). Plays by both of these authors led to theatre riots in Dublin over their representation of Irish society and politics, as when O'Casey depicted an Irish prostitute in *The Plough and the Stars* (1926) or showed a suspected informer pragmatically and coldly assassinated by the IRA in *Juno and the Paycock* (1924).

But in the first decade of the century, the contentious dramas were Synge's parables of cultural nationalism, such as *Riders to the Sea* (1904), which depicted Irish life unsullied by English colonialism, or *The Playboy of the Western World* (1907), a call to young Ireland to overthrow the tyranny of an oppressive father, who represents the religious and cultural backwardness of the Irish orthodoxy.

All of Ireland was ruled only from Westminster between 1801 and 1922. Within this period, the decisive phase of Irish resistance to English rule issued from the Celtic and Gaelic revivals of the late nineteenth century. Douglas Hyde founded the Gaelic League in 1893, positioning the real, anticolonial Ireland as essentially an agricultural community with a rural identity; meanwhile, Yeats embarked on his forging of an Irish identity based on Celtic culture, publishing his collection of folk stories, *The Celtic Twilight*, in the same year. Yeats attempted to instigate a new Irish poetry (with himself at the helm), a National Theatre, and a unifying Celtic mythology, amounting to a National Literary Revival. This began in 1897 with a declaration of intent agreed upon by Yeats, Lady Augusta Gregory and Edward Martyn to 'build up a Celtic and Irish school of dramatic literature' centred in Dublin. This was to be a new movement with a 'passion for oratory' and a 'freedom to experiment' not available 'in theatres of England'. With the establishment of the Irish National Theatre Society in 1902, the Celtic Renaissance was taken a step further.

Yeats's struggle culminated in his appeals to the Irish public in 1907 over *The Playboy of the Western World*, which provoked riots at the Abbey Theatre (superficially, at least, because a woman's shift was mentioned). In the play, a (fake) parricide is used to symbolize Ireland's need to attack the conventions and restrictions holding back its village communities: at the time it seemed to controversially suggest both that Irish women would be attracted by a hero who overthrew Ireland's patriarchal authorities and that violence could free the peasantry from imperial rule. In many ways, Synge, Yeats and James Joyce were all to become victims of the view that any depiction of the nation had to be a positive one, not simply one in opposition to that propagated by the English.

The Playboy of the Western World takes place near a village in County Mayo over the space of two days. The setting is a rough and ready country public house, or shebeen, and Synge writes in his introduction to the play that the words and phrases are drawn from conversations he has 'heard among the country people of Ireland', including the 'herds and fishermen' in Kerry and Mayo. Similarly, the ideas expressed in the play come from 'the folk-imagination'. Synge argued that the richness of his language resulted from his drama's source in the everyday expressions and opinions of people in the country who spoke naturally in a full-flavoured poetry with an organic vitality lacking in the city. For him, much modern drama had failed because it was divorced from common life, lacking both reality and joy.

The 'Western world' of the title refers to the north-west coast of island. In this wild and remote outpost beside the Atlantic, a young man called Christy bursts in one autumn evening to declare he has killed his father. The people in the public house are impressed by this announcement, and Christy is quarrelled over by the women and offered a job by the landlord protecting his whiskey from the English. Subsequent events focus on the return of Christy's father, courtship rivalries, and joyful living. The play ends with Christy heading off to enjoy an adventurous life, while Pegeen, the landlord's daughter, remarks on the difference between word and deed, but mourns the loss of 'the only Playboy of the Western world'. Blending poetic language with local dialect, the play is a powerful expression of peasant life and, consequently, Irish identity. In some way the public triumph of the Celtic Renaissance, it asserted the romance and charm of the West coast of Ireland, furthest distant from the English colonizers.

SHAW AND BRITISH DRAMA

The arrival of modernism in the British theatre is not usually thought to have happened in a significant way until Samuel Beckett's postwar plays, such as *Waiting for Godot*. However, earlier dramatists such as O'Casey and, in America, Eugene O'Neill introduced poetic and defamiliarizing elements to leaven drama's traditional realism.

Many critics have still seen the pretensions to verisimilitude of stage performance to work against modernist principles. This general but simple judgement ought to be qualified in several respects. Music, dance and review had brought radical techniques into the theatre, and Stravinsky's *The Rite of Spring* (1913) was one of the key cultural moments of the first decades of the twentieth century. The Norwegian dramatist Henrik Ibsen had revolutionized theatre singlehandedly and become the most influential playwright since Shakespeare. Other European dramatists from Chekhov and Strindberg, prewar, to Pirandello and Brecht, postwar, introduced irony, distancing effects, defamiliarization, symbolism and other modernist movements to drama.

In the London theatre, the most significant twentieth-century playwright, George Bernard Shaw (1856–1950), approached modernist techniques in his postwar dramas by using avant-garde effects, such as character reversal and defamiliarization techniques that undermined audience expectations. An Irish playwright, art critic, and socialist polemicist, Shaw thought the refusal to accept the anti-idealism and individualism advocated by Ibsen was possibly the biggest problem in modern civilization. Against claims of obscenity, Shaw wrote a defence of Ibsen called *The Quintessence of Ibsenism* early in his career, in 1891, and he became the most prominent champion of Ibsen's theatre and philosophy, rooted in the self-actualization of the individual against the subjugation and dictates of authority. Shaw's central argument was that there was a contemporary slavery to idealism and notions of 'goodness' against the quest for truth and aesthetic judgement. Shaw argued against censorship in the theatre and for Free Art, just as people accepted the principle of Free Trade. Shaw positioned Ibsen as a challenger of priggishness, duty and moral convention. Thus, Shaw particularly saw the Norwegian's plays in the light of his views on the emancipation of women, the overthrow of idealism (including democracy's reliance on subservience to the will of the majority), and the repudiation of conventional marriage and its duties. Shaw became a champion of other modernists, though he is not often seen as one himself, and his views on Ibsen and conventional morality echo the views of others, such as Nietzsche and Wagner, who Shaw also popularized.

An admirer of William Morris, Shaw was well-known as a Fabian, a socialist, a vegetarian and a proponent of rational dress. In the theatre, he was a radical in terms of content and form, even before the twentieth century. His first play, *Widowers' Houses* (1892), addresses slum landlords; he then wrote an unperformed comedy about Ibsenists called *The Philanderer*, followed by a play about prostitution that was banned, *Mrs Warren's Profession*. He opposed the approach of the common 'well-made play', introducing unresolved and surprising endings. Shaw's first considerable stage success was *John Bull's Other Island*, written at the invitation of W. B. Yeats for the Abbey Theatre in Dublin, but staged in 1904 by Granville Barker at London's Royal Court Theatre, which Shaw sponsored and supported. Shaw's position as the most seen and discussed dramatist in Britain developed with plays like *Androcles and the Lion* and *Misalliance* in the prewar years, when he also gained considerable international eminence. Shaw's work was extremely popular, but he was also politically outspoken and a radical at the centre of British theatre. His work veered more towards modernist sensibilities in the postwar years; his state-of-the-nation drama *Heartbreak House* (1919) lacks a plot or ending, and *Saint Joan* (1924) has an anti-realist epilogue in which the eponymous heroine and the other characters reappear after her death to discuss her martyrdom.

THREE LIVES (1909)

The American Gertrude Stein's *Three Lives* is an assembly of stories: 'The Good Anna', 'Melanctha', and 'The Gentle Lena'. It is unusual for the time in its comparatively frank portrayal of sexuality, ethnicity and mental health, but particularly in its formal qualities. Stein (1874–1946) studied under Henry James's brother, the philosopher and psychologist William James, at Radcliffe, and her influence on literature's portrayal of the workings of the mind is signally important. She enrolled at Johns Hopkins Medical School before giving up her studies and moving to Paris in 1903, not long before she started work on what would become *Three Lives*. She coined the expression 'Lost Generation' to describe many of the expatriate American writers who visited her in the city, where she lived until her death. She became a prolific writer in diverse genres, but all her work is characterized by fierce linguistic experimentation and an unwavering commitment to avant-garde principles.

In *Three Lives*, all three women, Anna, Melanctha and Lena, are ethnic outsiders who live frustrated and unfulfilled lives. The book's epigraph (supposedly from the French symbolist Laforgue) underlines its portrayal of lives of suffering brought about by natural inclination: 'So I am an unhappy person and this is neither my fault nor life's.' The implication is that Anna's goodness, Lena's gentleness, and something unnamed but divisive in Melanctha are the cause of their sorrowful lives and eventual deaths.

Three Lives is partly significant in terms of its depiction of sexuality, which includes implicit references to homoerotic love. Both lesbian and heterosexual ties are critiqued in the stories, and Stein repeatedly uses military and political imagery, portraying interpersonal relations in terms of descriptors like 'victory' and 'power'. Often this implies that Stein sees relationships as a struggle, whereby each lover is vying for supremacy. There is a less subtle implication in the text that marriage is like a prison sentence, or at least an institution that disempowers women, leaving them trapped with no prospect of 'escape.' Alternatives are no less easy, however, and Anna's relationship with, for example, Mrs Lehntman is only obliquely drawn, though 'Mrs. Lehntman was the only romance Anna ever knew.' The use of the word 'romance' implies a sexual connection between the two women, though again Stein is circumlocutious in her allusions to same-sex love. She is necessarily cautious, too, when describing Herman Kreder's homosexuality in the last of the stories, 'The Good Lena'.

In the second story of *Three Lives*, 'Melanctha', we see the influence of psychology and the development of Stein's radical thought after her studies under William James (who coined the term 'stream of consciousness'). Early in the story, Stein gives a long description of Melanctha, using repetition of her full name to reinforce the link between naming and character traits:

> Melanctha Herbert was always losing what she had in wanting all the things she saw. Melanctha was always being left when she was not leaving others.
>
> Melanctha Herbert always loved too hard and much too often. She was always full with mystery and subtle movements and denials and vague distrusts and complicated disillusions. Then Melanctha would be sudden and impulsive and unbounded in some faith, and then she would suffer and be strong in her repression. (Stein: 60)

There is a sense here of strength, but deep inner tension, culminating in the word 'repression' which stretches towards both Freudian and political meanings. Again intimating an inner life that most novels of the period would barely sketch, in 'The Gentle Lena' Stein outlines Lena's deterioration into mental illness, which, it is implied, is a result of the way in which her mother-in-law is treating her:

> There's that poor Lena, she just been here crying and looking so careless so I scold her, but that was no good that marrying for that

poor Lena, Mrs. Aldrich. She do look so pale and sad now Mrs. Aldrich, it just break my heart to see her ... and now she got to stand it all the time with that old woman Mrs. Kreder. My! Mrs. Aldrich, she is a bad old woman to her. (Stein: 180)

Lena's 'madness' is suggestively symbolic of repressed sexuality, and the way in which she is 'used' by her mother-in-law, revealing a more complicated relationship between the mind and body than is usually evident in the realist novel.

Three Lives also both reinforces and subverts racial stereotypes, especially in 'Melanctha'. At times, a character such as Rose asserts her identity as an African American, but at others Stein's descriptive language portrays the historical context as one of systematic denigration of the black characters, and Rose is repeatedly portrayed in unnatural or animalistic terms.

Stein was a radical lesbian feminist, and her presentation of gender is also complex. In 'Melanctha' the main character's voice is chiefly mediated by the male voice of Jeff Campbell, her lover, having the effect of almost silencing her throughout the story. She is given a perspective through her debates with him, but there is the constant sense of mediation and the reader has to unearth Melanctha's sense of being within and between the lines.

As important is Stein's interest in complex literary form. Her writing has been likened to cubism, an art form she influenced, in its abandoning of a single, fixed viewpoint for a multiplicity of angles, presenting an accumulated multisided image of a character or situation. So in *Three Lives* Stein uses multiple perspectives among other formal qualities. We not only see the narrative from the point of view of the protagonist, but from those of other characters. This builds layered perspectives on the character, as though Stein is building up layers of paint on a canvas, slowly constructing and reinforcing or varying our sense of identity. Stein was influenced at this time by the artist Paul Cézanne, whose attention to detail and whose faux-naïf approach to art allowed her to begin *Three Lives* as a new kind of writing, indebted to repetition and digression. In her use of the continuous present tense, in keeping with Henri Bergson's concept of time's duration in the mind and William James's idea of the stream of consciousness, there is no linear progression through time in the narrative, but instead a succession of moments that surround consciousness.

'Melanctha' is the story that has drawn most critical attention, partly because it is the most formally experimental, shaping its prose according to the character's mental processes, but also because of its repeated sexual imagery and innuendo combined with its imaginative, if problematic, engagement with issues of ethnicity. Like Picasso's use of African masks in his painting, the adoption or appropriation of a black mask allowed Stein, in 'Melanctha' to flout the styles and conventions she wished to escape in order to represent fully both her life and a new twentieth-century form of writing. *Three Lives* arguably heralds a change in style from realist to pointedly 'experimental' models of writing in its use of 'subjective' or oblique narrators, the juxtaposition of considered reason and emotional urgency, more natural speech patterns, and the shift to inwardness, or from the conscious to the unconscious.

Contemporary reviewers thought her style was characterized by 'a detailed showing of the repeated thoughts in the brain' and 'repetitions, false starts, and general circularity'. Critics have since concluded that this stylization is the start of Stein's progress toward a kind of writing utterly concerned with the formal features of language: an abstract, self-contained, plastic, autonomous literature.

HOWARDS END (1910) AND
THE CONDITION OF ENGLAND (1909)

E. M. Forster's *Howards End* has partly become famous for its epigraph, 'Only connect', which stands as a call across Forster's writing to seize the day and unite the spiritual and the material sides to life, seeing human existence both clearly and wholly. His fourth novel is a story of two families, the entrepreneurial Wilcoxes and the intellectual Schlegels.

The Wilcoxes are a male-dominated, middle-class family with a successful domestic and imperial business. They stand for industry and finance, commerce and capital: an outer life of 'telegrams and anger' that embodies the Protestant work ethic and masculine endeavour (Forster 1975: 41). The Schlegels – Margaret, Helen and Tibby – are young, sensitive, and cerebral Londoners of German descent. They cherish the 'inner world' of personal relationships and humane liberal culture.

Forster suggests in the novel that while he more highly values the conscience-driven life of the Schlegels, he recognizes that they cannot survive without the ambitious industry of the Wilcoxes. Their worlds are contrasted in many ways in the narrative, but Forster believes they are both important. For example, they favour different modes of modern transport: the train and the automobile. The Wilcoxes are forever charging around in their motorcars, private vehicles that rush them past or even over everything in their way. By contrast, Forster describes the way in which London's public railways and their stations appear, to Margaret, to encompass all of Britain:

> She had strong feelings about the various railway termini. They are our gates to the glorious and the unknown. Through them we pass out into adventure and sunshine, to them, alas! we return. In Paddington all Cornwall is latent and the remoter west; down the inclines of Liverpool Street lie fenlands and the illimitable Broads; Scotland is through the pylons of Euston; Wessex behind the poised chaos of Waterloo.... To Margaret ... the station of King's Cross had always suggested infinity. (Forster 1975: 27)

The drawing of the disparity between the two families makes *Howards End* a highly schematic novel. At the heart of its vision of England and the need to connect people lies the spirit of the totemic Mrs Wilcox (born Ruth Howard), who smoothes over disagreements and remains calmly serene. When the families meet again in London, Margaret and Mrs Wilcox develop a brief but firm friendship. Mrs Wilcox attends one of the Schlegels' free-thinking lunch parties at which young intellectuals congregate to discuss contemporary social issues and ideas, but which she finds abstract and unengaging. After Margaret has helped her with her Christmas shopping, Mrs Wilcox urgently wishes her to go to Howards End, Mrs Wilcox's family home, with which she feels the elder Miss Schlegel has a sympathetic spiritual link. Meanwhile, Helen has introduced another slightly fraught friendship into the family through a casual but awkward encounter with a young clerk, the self-improving Leonard Bast. Forster portrays Bast as the victim of the modern city, in which he suffers physical hardship while hoping to become cultured, though the Schlegels want to see him living a more authentic rural life. The first half of the novel ends surprisingly, with Mrs Wilcox's unexpected death and, in the light of her knowledge that the Schlegels are shortly to lose the home they were born in, her final wish that

Margaret inherit Howards End. The Wilcox family members discuss, but refuse to acknowledge, this deathbed request.

Two years later, when the families meet again, the Schlegels ask Mr Wilcox for advice over how they should help the struggling Bast. Wilcox suggests that Leonard change jobs, as his present employer appears to be in financial trouble. This advice leads to Leonard becoming unemployed, for which Helen blames Mr Wilcox. Margaret, meanwhile, has made an impression on Wilcox and, on the pretext of finding her a house, he develops a friendship with her and then makes a proposal of marriage, which she accepts.

Mr Wilcox and Margaret marry and the Schlegels' property from their old London address is stored at Howards End. Here, the furniture is unpacked and installed in the cottage by an old friend of the first Mrs Wilcox who is looking after the vacant property. When Helen returns to England and goes to Howards End for some of her belongings, Mr Wilcox and Margaret discover that she is pregnant by Leonard Bast. The following morning, Leonard arrives at Howards End and is set upon by an indignant Charles Wilcox, Mr Wilcox's elder son. Though only struck lightly with the side of a sword, Leon ard collapses under a falling bookcase, suffers a heart attack and dies. For his assault, Charles receives a verdict of manslaughter and is sent to prison, an even greater scandal for the family than Helen's pregnancy. Mr Wilcox has a nervous breakdown and Margaret decides to look after him, as well as Helen, at Howards End.

Several months later, Helen has had a baby boy, Mr Wilcox decides to give Howards End to the Schlegels, and Margaret finally learns that Mrs Wilcox had in fact intended to bequeath the property to her when she died. Thus, through a complicated story, Leonard and Helen's child will come to inherit Howards End, which Forster holds up as a symbol of England throughout the narrative.

The novel overall works as a condition-of-the-nation story, in which the question of which section of the middle-class best represents the country is debated: the commercial, commonsensical Wilcoxes; the cultured, progressive Schlegels; or the new urban yeomanry represented by Leonard. The diagrammatic nature of the novel works both to follow this question through in an organized, imaginative way, but perhaps also to undermine the reader's sense of the events' credibility. Regarded by some as Forster's best book, it is in most ways a discursive and allegorical text, quite different from the symbolist style of what is arguably Forster's only foray into modernism, *A Passage to India*.

However, the separation between culture and economics within society is a major theme of *Howards End* and arguably indicates one sense in which, though the book is in many ways realist, Forster's social analysis reaches towards a modernist sensibility in the novel, and on occasion his style does, too. For example, Cyril Connolly wrote in his 1938 survey of modern literature, *Enemies of Promise*, that *Howards End* constituted a revolutionary break from the writing of the nineteenth century. Published only a few years before the Great War, at a time when the suffragette movement was active and class divisions were accentuated by the rise of trade unions, it is important that the novel's organization and outlook rest upon a division between the male, practical, English Wilcoxes and the female, artistic, German Schlegels, in which the former have power and money while the latter have culture and social pedigree. The differences between the two families are better seen in terms of mental attitudes than material ones, with Leonard Bast caught in the middle and condemned as a victim of urbanization because his yeoman stock belongs in the country, where his child will be raised. Forster is most interested in the spiritual values of England and Englishness, and with the question of who should inherit Howards End. The theme of 'only connect' is particularly relevant to Margaret's attempt to get Mr Wilcox to see that Helen's affair with Leonard is paralleled by Mr Wilcox's earlier affair with Jacky Bast, but it also reflects on the situation at the end of the novel, in which Wilcox property, Schlegel sensibilities, and Bast genes are combined at Howards End to raise Helen's baby. *Howards End*'s wider context is thus provided by books published around the same time with broadly similar concerns, particularly the liberal politician C. F. G. Masterman's 1909 study *The Condition of England* and H. G. Wells's most critically admired novel *Tono-Bungay*, from the same year.

Partly inspired by Wells's vision of a society threatened by social disintegration and fragmentation, Masterman's book begins with a preface that opens with a quotation from *Tono-Bungay*: 'I've got to a time of life when the only theories that interest me are generalisations about realities.' Masterman says that his book is an attempt 'to estimate some of these "realities" in the life of contemporary England.' As such, it is sometimes seen as a political, religious and social state-of-the-nation study to sit alongside Wells's novel about a miracle cure that is, in fact, just a soft drink. In no small part based on the story of Coca-Cola, Wells's novel was the one he considered his finest, which he described in his 1925 preface as 'a view of the contemporary social and political system in Great Britain, an old and degenerating system, tried and strained by new inventions and new ideas'. It was subtitled when first serialized as 'A Study of Commerce' but is as much a lament for the 'cancerous' and 'tumourous' growth of the city, similarly lamented in *Howards End* as the red rust of the metropolis taking over the country(side), and the scramble for African resources that is paralleled by the Wilcoxes' Imperial and West African rubber company.

A novel of the middle classes, with little to say about the upper and lower sections of society, *Howards End* nevertheless remains an important study of the 'death of Liberal England' and of the twilight years before the Great War. It is evidently an anxious book about change and transition, like contemporary works by Wells and Lawrence, but it is also a novel intimately and illuminatingly concerned with the connections between private and public worlds. With the possible exception of Conrad's best work, it ranks alongside any other twentieth-century English novel published before 1914, and its concern with the modern forces encroaching on familiar patterns of living places it in the line of critiques connecting Hardy, who spoke of the incipient 'ache of modernism' to Lawrence, who dramatized its effects.

EDWARDIANS AND GEORGIANS

The novelists that came to be considered modernist were not, for the most part, commercially successful in their own time. The authors who did sell well were also on occasion the subject of the modernists' admiration or criticism. The novels of three British writers in particular were discussed by modernists in their essays, letters, and reviews: John Galsworthy (1867–1933), H. G. Wells (1866–1946), and Arnold Bennett (1867–1931). At the time, the term 'modernist' was not in use, but another brace of terms was suggested by a watershed moment in May 1910, when Victoria's son King Edward VII died, and the Prince of Wales ascended to the throne, becoming King George V. This signalled a shift, at least in terms of available rhetoric, from 'Edwardian' to 'Georgian': from an old guard to a younger generation.

In well-known plays such as *Strife* (1909), Galsworthy tackled social and class issues in the Edwardian era, but it is for his novels that he is now better known, particularly the long series of fictions that comprise *The Forsyte Saga*, starting with *The Man of Property* (1906). An heir to Dickens and Kipling, Arnold Bennett was probably the most respected novelist of the Edwardian era, his reputation building after the publication of *The Old Wives' Tale* in 1908 and his success touring America. His early desire to join the literary elite was soon swapped for a pragmatic approach to writing after the commercial failure of his first novel, so he turned to the most profitable aspects of journalism, reviewing educational books and then sagas, such as the *Clayhanger* series (1910–18). Like Galsworthy and Bennett, H. G. Wells was an indefatigable writer, responsible for dozens of works in many genres. He is now best known for his 1890s science fiction romances, such as *The Time Machine* and *The War of the Worlds*, but he also wrote social realist novels, notably *Kipps* (1905), *Tono-Bungay* (1909) and *The History of Mr Polly* (1910). Several publications in one year were the norm for such writers, who in some ways saw a critique of Victorian and Edwardian social ills as their main aim, rather than an experimental engagement with literary form, though they were deeply concerned with the state of the novel.

Wells debated the role of fiction as art or entertainment with Henry James. An admirer, James still felt that Wells insufficiently considered the value of the knowledge, facts and details he was painstakingly unearthing. James believed that novels by Wells or Arnold Bennett were remarkable for their 'quarried and gathered material' but that little scrutiny of the detail followed from its accumulation. Facts were foregrounded at the expense of analysis and consideration. Denouncing what he saw as an art-for-art's-sake spirit, Wells criticized James in a semi-autobiographical novel, *Boon* (1915), for seeing art as an end rather than a means. Wells would rather, he said, be called a journalist than an artist. James replied in two letters, saying, 'It is art that *makes* life, makes interest, makes importance'. For Wells, fiction worked towards the ends not of art, but of education, social criticism and entertainment. It was art for a purpose, like architecture, whereas James's fiction was not, like painting. James contested the distinction, believing all art was for a purpose that was aesthetically determined. Wells had fashioned his own view of James's overreverence for artistic construction, saying his fiction was 'like a church lit but without a congregation to distract you, with every light and line focussed on the high altar. And on the altar, very reverently placed, intensely there, is a dead kitten, an egg-shell, a bit of string' (See Ellmann and Feidelson: 317–28).

Virginia Woolf included Wells as one of her 'materialists' who she thought see life only from the outside, not from within. This was a term she used in two well-known essays in which she criticized the fiction of the popular serious novelists of the time. Woolf singled out Bennett, who James also attacked for writing novels without principles of organization, such that they resembled 'fluid pudding'. The dispute lasted from 1917 until Bennett's death in 1931. Woolf's first essay is entitled 'Modern Fiction' (1919). It upbraids the 'materialists' for writing about 'unimportant things', making the transitory appear enduring and important, reversing on Wells the accusation he levelled at James. Woolf admired the industry of Bennett and Wells, but thought: 'Life escapes: and perhaps without life nothing else is worthwhile'. For Woolf, 'life' meant the inner world: psychology, character and thought, desire and memory: 'Life is not a series of gig-lamps symmetrically arranged but a luminous halo, a semi-transparent envelope surrounding us from the beginning of consciousness to the end. Is it not the task of the novelist to convey this varying, this unknown and uncircumscribed spirit, whatever aberration or complexity it may display, with as little mixture of the alien and external as possible?' (Woolf 1919: 123).

Woolf's other often quoted essay is 'Mr Bennett and Mrs Brown' (1924), in which she stated unequivocally that 'in or about December, 1910, human character changed.' She was principally referring to the representation of human nature in art and its understanding. Her target here was Arnold Bennett, while she argued her belief that the novel's purpose was to represent character. Bennett, in fact, agreed with this, and conversely felt that the Georgians (Forster, Lawrence, Joyce) did not construct characters who were 'real, true and convincing', while the Edwardians (himself, Wells and Galsworthy) had depicted believable people living in recognizable communities. Illustrating that the disagreement between them was about *how* character should best be presented, rather than the relative prominence of character and plot, Woolf agreed: 'Bennett convinces us so well that there is a house, in every detail, that we become convinced that there must be a person living there.' The disagreement, for Woolf, hinged on how to describe the representative figure of Mrs Brown, a woman sitting in a railway carriage. Bennett, she decided, would list every aspect of Mrs Brown's dress and appearance while delivering copious extra details about her life, without taking the reader into Mrs Brown's mind. For Woolf, therefore, it could be said that with the advent of the Georgian period, because literary approaches had changed, human character had changed.

To complete this picture of opposed generations, it can be noted that Galsworthy also drew the ire and opprobrium of D. H. Lawrence, who thought he wrote 'documentary fictions' with characters 'lacking a "real being"'. Lawrence wrote an essay on Galsworthy in 1927, which was published the following year. In the essay he says that not one of Galsworthy's characters "seems to be a really vivid human being.' ('John Galsworthy' in *Phoenix*). He saw them instead as socially defined: 'the whole necessity for thus materially insuring oneself with wealth, money, arises from the state of fear into which a man falls who has lost his at-oneness with the living universe'. Lawrence saw these characters defined by money or property, and while Galsworthy portrayed them as parasites for the reader to understand in this negative light, there was nothing but 'degraded social beings' in the novels, defined by the vulgar, sentimental and cynical. He also thought that Galsworthy had deteriorated as an artist as he grew older, underlining once again a generational divide: 'The later novels are purely commercial, and, if it had not been for the early novels, of no importance. They are popular, they sell well, and there's the end of them.' More recently, the reputations of Wells, Bennett, and Galsworthy have risen again as their social foresight, critical acumen, and literary abilities have been rerecognized. They suffered from being positioned as stalking horses for the avant-garde to attack, but they were in many ways progressive writers, whose focus on the social world now seems more valuable than it did to the modernist writers or their twentieth-century critics.

CHAPTER TWO

1910s

INTRODUCTION

The Great War hangs over the 1910s to such an extent that its impact seems to reach back to the start of the decade. The years from 1910 to 1914 are seen as the last gasp of a confident Imperial Edwardian summer in Britain, felt most strongly in the long days of sunshine in 1914 that stretched from the assassination of Archduke Ferdinand of Austria at the end of June to the declaration of war on August 3. Readings of the decade may also seem masculinist in their emphasis on war, but the social background is marked by battles of gender.

The fight for the vote by women, up to 1918 in Britain and 1920 in the United States, is a crucial social and cultural aspect to the period. The main political interests used to mask this internal political gender division, British Imperialism and national identity, also excluded women. In her 1938 book *Three Guineas*, Virginia Woolf was to argue that women were still positioned outside a masculine patriotism that had appropriated English identity. As mentioned at the end of Chapter One, in her 1924 essay 'Mr Bennett and Mrs Brown' Woolf also famously stated that 'On or about December 1910 human character changed'. Among other things, she was referring to the 1910 London art exhibition entitled 'Manet and the Post-Impressionists' curated by her fellow Bloomsburyite Roger Fry. Fry's exhibition was shocking for many art goers who had never seen examples of abstract and experimental work before. Fine art was preceding literature in the sense of breaking moulds and forging new forms, such as cubism, expressionism and the design of art deco, but in the 1910s poetry and prose would begin to reflect this new aesthetic sensibility.

The modernist short story comes to fruition in this decade, too, with the publication of first volumes by Katherine Mansfield and James Joyce. In the modernist novel, the key names are Joyce, Ford and Conrad again, with writers like Virginia Woolf, D. H. Lawrence and Wyndham Lewis making a new impact as critics as well as writers. Driven by circles surrounding such figures as Pound, Lewis, Ford and the Bloomsbury set, these were formative years of a new aesthetic sensibility that showed a desire for change that ran in parallel to that in politics. The war would crystallize this energy into a more radical modernism in the 1920s, but the sense of urgency developed in the decade before.

THE 'LITTLE MAGAZINES'

As is apparent from the discussion of Conrad's novels in Chapter One, serial publication in magazines was normal for novels in the first decades of the century. Publication was often in long-established weeklies or monthlies, but there were also numerous new and esoteric literary publications. Particularly in America, modernism thrived in what became known as 'little magazines'. An intellectual culture flourished in journals alongside a newness in urban living, from the skyscraper office block and the assembly line, to jazz and modern transport. The little magazines aimed to create a readership for experimental work, to foster the circulation of new ideas, and to be a vehicle for the promotion of important, but less commercial, literature. Some important examples were *The Dial* (1916), *The Little Review* (1914), *The Seven Arts* (1916) and *Contact* (1920), but there were dozens that started up and lasted from one edition to many decades. One key publication still thrives today: *Poetry: A Magazine of Verse* was founded in 1912 by a Chicago poet called Harriet Monroe to provide an outlet for the work of new poets. A well-connected art critic, she was able to enlist the patronage of over 100 investors. The magazine quickly established a position as the pre-eminent outline for modern and experimental verse. Showcasing works from the Chicago Literary Renaissance, it went on to gather early contributions from Wallace Stevens, Marianne Moore, D. H. Lawrence, Robert Frost and William Carlos Williams. T. S. Eliot's 'The Love Song of J. Alfred Prufrock' was published by the magazine in 1915 when its foreign correspondent, Ezra Pound, brought Eliot to attention. The magazine was a support and sponsor to original

poetry, rather than just an outlet, and it was responsible for transforming perceptions of both literary value and poetic experimentation. Monroe stated her editorial policy of the magazine as follows:

> The Open Door will be the policy of this magazine – may the great
> poet we are looking for never find it shut, or half-shut, against his
> ample genius! To this end the editors hope to keep free from entan-
> gling alliances with any single class or school. They desire to print
> the best English verse which is being written today, regardless of
> where, by whom, or under what theory of art it is written. Nor will
> the magazine promise to limit its editorial comments to one set of
> opinions.

Other key magazines in England included Pound and Wyndham
Lewis's launch in 1914 of *BLAST*, a short-lived vorticist experiment
in declaration, art, typography and literature, and *The New Freewoman*. The latter began in 1911 as *The Freewoman*, launched by
Dora Marsden as a women's suffragette magazine. It soon evolved
into a vehicle for modernist works, and Marsden eventually changed
the name to *The Egoist*, because she believed women should cultivate
their self-esteem. May Sinclair, Lawrence and Eliot were all contributors, but the magazine is best known for serializing Joyce's *A Portrait of
the Artist as a Young Man* and *Ulysses* under the editorship of Harriet
Shaw Weaver. *The Waste Land* was first published in the journals *The
Criterion* and *The Dial*, and it is an important aspect to understanding the contemporary context to publication that it was without notes
or the other poems that appeared alongside it in book form. *BLAST*
ran to only two issues, the inaugural edition in June 1914 and a July
1915 'War Issue'. The first publication foregrounded a vorticist manifesto rejecting futurism and imagism, lambasting the rich and the
poor, and offering BLASTS and BLESSINGS. These were aimed at
tackling the art, poetry, politics and popular consciousness of England
in the 1910s as the 'great art vortex sprung up'. Contributors included
Lewis, Eliot, Ford Madox Ford and Rebecca West.

The avant-garde element in the little magazines continued throughout the modernist period, and, for example, *transition* published its
twelve declarations as 'The Revolution of the Word', including 'The
revolution of the English Language is an accomplished fact', 'Time is a
tyranny to be abolished', 'The writer expresses. He does not communicate' and 'The plain reader be damned.' Modernism's reputation for

difficulty cannot be separated from these kinds of sentiments, typical of the proliferating manifestos that proclaimed the death of one thing along with the birth of another, often using bold colours, striking typefaces or fonts, and coloured paper.

For the reader today, works of modernism appear in books and anthologies, but many essays, poems and even novels first appeared in journals, and the 'little magazines' are as much a part of modernism's historical context as the triple-decker and the serialization are to the nineteenth-century novel. Renewed interest in the culture of 'little magazines' has also been linked with efforts to reassert the role of women in modernism, which has been presented in the past in terms of not only predominantly male writers, but also intermediaries. Women were more instrumental in the evolution of modernism than is generally acknowledged. The importance of Monroe and her first coeditor of *Poetry*, Alice Corbin Henderson, can be supplemented by Margaret Anderson and Jane Heap, editors of the *Little Review* (1914–29), and the poet Marianne Moore, editor of *The Dial* (1925–29). There were, in fact, many dozens of little magazines in the early part of the twentieth century and these were the main distributors of avant-garde work at a time when inexpensive paperbacks were not yet available and access to new literature relied on this kind of periodical publication, which had the added benefit of providing extensive networks of both writers and readers. Thus, Arthur Kreymborg's *Others: A Magazine of the New Verse* (1915–19) celebrated its American modernist departure from the European traditions, publishing Mina Loy, William Carlos Williams, Louise Bogan and others who announced their arrival on the modernist scene, with other contributions coming from Wallace Stevens, Marianne Moore, Ezra Pound, Conrad Aiken, Carl Sandburg, T. S. Eliot, Amy Lowell, H. D. and Djuna Barnes.

The culture of the little magazine rested on a strong and pioneering spirit that brought out the best in Anglo-American interfusions. British modernist writers were spurred by overseas influences of all kinds from around the globe, but it was writers like James, Pound, Eliot and Stein who epitomized an American new world spirit rejuvenating old world sensibilities; a theme common in many modernist novels, too.

BEGINNINGS OF IMAGISM

The first examples of imagism in general circulation were three short poems by H. D. (Hilda Doolittle) published in Chicago in 1912 by

Monroe's *Poetry* magazine, but the movement perhaps gained its greatest impetus with the move to Europe in 1908 of H. D.'s friend from the University of Philadelphia, Ezra Pound, who lived first in Venice, but settled in London. Another of the impetuses for imagism came in 1909 from a group in Soho that surrounded the ideas and person of the critic and poet T. E. Hulme. Of particular direct importance at the Poets' Club was a paper Hulme gave towards the end of 1908 called A Lecture on Modern Poetry, which argued influentially for free verse.

The principles of the imagist movement were laid down by Pound as 'A Few Don'ts by An Imagist' though he chose not to remain among the group when the movement developed. Pound cultivated H. D.'s poetry when she arrived in London from America in 1911, and along with Richard Aldington, the three of them were declared 'imagistes' by Pound. His manifesto of their beliefs advocated precise advice intended for the new poet, such as to avoid abstraction, rhetoric and ornamentation. Central is the emphasis on studying the tradition and working laboriously to know the history of poetry, but not to write in the modes of the past: reinvention and making art anew, was vital. Only three principles were agreed upon by the original three imagists, however:

(1) Direct treatment of the 'thing,' whether subjective or objective.
(2) To use absolutely no word that does not contribute to the presentation.
(3) As regarding rhythm: to compose in the sequence of the musical phrase, not in sequence of a metronome.

Imagism had many of its roots in the circle of thinkers surrounding T. E. Hulme, who Pound had gotten to know in 1908, and in French philosophical literature, especially the symbolist poets such as Verlaine and Villon. The movement could also be characterized as a rejection of Victorian poetry and an embrace of classical, especially Greek, literature, which H. D. and Aldington had been translating. Under Pound's championing, imagism became highly influential on both sides of the Atlantic and its close attention to language is often thought to have instigated modernist poetry. Forging a connection between English and American writers, through the intermediary work of writers such as Pound, was also a major contribution of the Imagists to the development of modernism through the interfusion of ideas. This cross-pollination was also enhanced by the migration of writers such as James, Stein and Eliot to Europe, making London and then Paris hubs of intellectual activity.

Imagism, as Pound first delineated it, sees the poem as a complex in which 'painting or sculpture seems as if it were just coming over into speech'. Pound chose as exemplary H. D.'s poem 'Oread':

Whirl up, sea –
whirl your pointed pines,
splash your great pines
on our rocks
hurl your green over us,
cover us with your pools of fir.

For some critics, imagism derives most clearly from Hulme's earlier impressionist school, reshaped into Pound's creed of the image. In particular, Hulme advocated a return to classicism against a prevailing nineteenth-century spirit of romanticism with its abstract imagery, intense emotion and transcendent ideology. Imagism, instead, was to find the right vivid but concrete metaphors to present 'small, dry things'. Influenced by Oriental poetry, Pound commonly favoured juxtaposition, hard images and succinct metaphorical formulations, such as he used in the two-line poem 'In a Station of the Metro':

The apparition of these faces in the crowd;
Petals on a wet, black bough.

Much subsequent criticism sees imagism perhaps less as important poetry in itself and more as a call to revolution for English language poetry in general, using techniques that might be characterized as simplicity, directness and sparseness. Its significance in this way is considerable, and is akin to that of cubism in art, but its insistence on a certain kind of poetry and subject was ultimately an inevitable limiting factor that was overly prescriptive and ignored other potential avenues for poetry's development.

For the most part, the poets used *vers libre*, allowing a freedom of verse that accompanied the rigorous principles of abjuring abstractions, seeking concentration, and avoiding superfluous words in order to write crystalline poetry: hard and clear. There is thus little emotional content in most imagist poetry, but often a visual comparison between two phenomena. The influence can also be seen in canonical modernist poems such as Eliot's 'The Love Song of J. Alfred Prufrock' and 'The Waste Land', which utilize less concrete imagery, but often make striking comparisons that are unexpected and intriguing, such as in the former: 'I should have been a pair of ragged claws / Scuttling across the floors of silent seas.'

A collection was published as *Des Imagistes* in 1914. Pound saw the volume as a way to advertise and promote his new movement, but by the time of publication he had moved on to a new interest in vorticism. H.D., Richard Aldington and Amy Lowell, whose involvement Pound had resented, decided to continue with an annual publication and so produced *Some Imagist Poets* in the following three years. These volumes were conceived on the basis that they would include selections chosen by the poets, while Aldington amplified the dictums of the movement in terms of a complete freedom of subject, the Flaubertian deployment of the 'exact word' and the Wordsworthian use of 'common speech'. Aldington's war service interrupted the movement's development to a degree, but the volumes had brought to wider attention the work of many important modernist figures, including D. H. Lawrence, William Carlos Willams and Ford Madox Ford. A final imagist anthology was produced in 1930 as modernism itself was losing impetus, with several of its key figures dead (Lawrence and Lowell) or ploughing different furrows.

CHARLOTTE MEW

There are many underconsidered female authors of the early and high modernist period. These include writers such as Charlotte Mew, Anna Wickham, Alice Meynell and Edith Sitwell. In this section, as an example, I will discuss Charlotte Mew (1869–1928), who wrote stories, essays and overtly feminist poetry that was approvingly reviewed and acknowledged in its day, but less so in the subsequent decades of the twentieth century. Mew's poetry is notable for its political analyses of mental health, femininity, ecology, prostitution and war. There is also a sexual frankness and ambiguity in her poetry, unexpectedly rendered in formal verse alongside modernist technique, including rhymed free verse.

With a considerable history of mental illness in her family, Mew wrote about 'madness' and disability in several poems including 'On the Asylum Road' and 'Ken'. The latter has been thought a reaction to the 1913 Mental Deficiency Act, which defined grades of mental 'defect' and how they should be 'dealt with' by Boards of Control. The speaker's attitude to Ken at the beginning of the poem is of curiosity and puzzlement. He is presented as the 'other':

> When first I came upon him there
> Suddenly, on the half-lit stair,
> I think I hardly found a trace
> Of likeness to a human face
>   In his. And I said then
> If in His image God made men
> Some other must have made poor Ken –
> But for his eyes which looked at you
> As two red, wounded stars might do.
>   (See Roberts and Falkenberg for all of Mew's texts.)

The man is not seen as totally human at the beginning of the stanza: the speaker cannot see 'a trace / Of likeness to a human face / In his.' It is interesting, too, that there is a line break after 'face' so that he is literally detached from humanity within the form of the poem. However, there is some poignancy to this description in that his eyes are like 'red, wounded stars' – the speaker is conscious of his suffering. The conclusion of the poem – its last three stanzas – tells of Ken's incarceration in an asylum. They begin with the speaker pondering the lack of freedom for its patients:

> But in that red brick barn upon the hill
>   I wonder – can one own the deer,
> And does one walk with children still
>   As one did here –
>   Do roses grow
> Beneath those twenty windows in a row –
>
>   And if some night
> When you have not seen any light
> They cannot move you from your chair
>   What happens there?
>   I do not know.

The idea of the asylum is immediately associated with the reduction of its patients to a herd of animals, kept locked in a 'red brick barn' and away from other human contact, 'upon the hill'. The speaker has to imagine what occurs in these places, but it is done rhetorically, and with some irony, in the context of the rest of the poem. The descriptions consist of Ken's activities when he was living in the community, and raise questions of how just it is to remove someone from this community and forcibly place them in an asylum. The speaker's use of pronouns for the patient has also changed from the third to the second person, addressing not the reader, but Ken as 'you'. Such interest in the care and treatment of traumatized men was, of course, to become a major concern in discussions of shell shock during and after the war, for example in Rebecca West's *The Return of the Soldier* and Woolf's *Mrs Dalloway*, but Mew's poem demonstrates a female literary interest in the subject that could be connected back to patriarchal treatments of the 'female malady' of 'hysteria' in the nineteenth century.

Some of Mew's most intriguing work is contained in her prose, such as the essays 'Men and Trees I,' 'Men and Trees II' (1913) and the story 'A White Night' (1903), seen by Elaine Showalter as a 'feminist counterpart to Conrad's apocalyptic *Heart of Darkness.*' (Showalter xvii) In 'Men and Trees I' and 'Men and Trees II,' Mew offers a polemical account of the importance of trees in relation to people; she places them in their historical and cultural contexts, using quotations from literary sources to support her ideas. The first essay begins with Mew discussing the disappearance of trees in London, which makes her argument perhaps more relevant to her reader:

> The London trees are all prisoners of men, some unreasonably mutilated like the lopped crowd in Greenwich Park, while, now and then, there is a wholesale massacre such as that of the seven hundred in Kensington Gardens, which took place, no one knows why, some thirty years ago, against which even the executioners protested and perhaps the homeless rooks as vainly. In my own wooded neighbourhood one after another falls; progress pulls down the old spacious shabby houses and puts up flats for the half-world.

Mew's use of personification in her descriptions – 'trees are all prisoners of men' that have been 'mutilated' and 'massacre[d]' – allows the reader to identify with their plight and connect the human with the arboreal. The choice of diction is very stark, even shocking, in the use of violent imagery. Mew's language suggests a deep conscious-ness of the importance to human life of ecosystems, and of their interrelationship. She is mourning the loss of trees to 'progress,' which suggests a disparaging attitude towards the urbanization that occurred in the early twentieth century, and an antipathy to the grow-ing industrialization that accompanied it.

In the second of the essays, 'Men and Trees II,' Mew talks in some-what different terms from Conrad in *Heart of Darkness* about the tribespeople of the Congo, and how the destruction of trees for their rubber has had disastrous consequences:

> These, of course, are the darker superstitions; civilization, brightly conscious of having abolished the devils with the gods, and replaced them all by the *Culte du Moi*, murmurs 'shocking!' and hurries on; but there is not much doubt that human sacrifices are still being offered by American and European syndicates to the sacred tree of civilization, the rubber tree. Civilization demands speed, speed demands rubber, and rubber, coated with blood and slime, turns quickly into gold. We have almost forgotten the Congo, and the whole story of the unique and more hideous abominations of the Putumayo is not yet and probably never will be told. So far we know that within ten years the greater part of a gay, intelligent native race has been monstrously exploited and destroyed.

Mew preempts the postmodernist concern with recentering margin-alized narratives and, at the same time, she acknowledges that this story may never 'be told' in full. Her anger at the West's hypocrisy is implied in the first few lines of the quotation, which culminates in an ironic and stark description: 'Civilization demands speed, speed demands rubber, and rubber, coated with blood and slime, turns quickly into gold.' The suggestion is that it is human, and perhaps also animal, 'blood' that is spilled for financial gain, the cost of capitalism.

The first and most important collection of Mew's poems, *The Farmer's Bride*, was issued in 1916 by Monro's Poetry Bookshop. The poems in this collection focus on lost love and emotional denial, quite possibly because Mew feared the hereditary mental instability in her family, and her poems deal not with family life or with the traditional poetic subjects but with peddlers, changelings and the marginalized. The speaker in 'The Farmer's Bride', her most famous poem, is the farmer himself. This poem opens by telling of a woman's submission to male dominance but one night in autumn she escapes her husband:

> 'Out 'mong the sheep, her be,' they said,
> 'Should properly have been abed;
> But sure enough she wasn't there
> Lying awake with her wide brown stare.
> So over seven-acre field and up-along across the down
> We chased her, flying like a hare
> Before our lanterns. To Church-Town
> All in a shiver and a scare
> We caught her, fetched her home at last
> And turned the key upon her, fast.

The farmer constructs his wife as childlike, mad and animallike, implied by the following descriptions respectively: 'Should properly have been abed', 'her wide brown stare', and 'We chased her, flying like a hare'. It is as though he envisages himself as a parent or a guardian, rather than a husband. The last two lines of this stanza emphasize this further, as well as highlighting his patriarchal attitude: 'We caught her, fetched her home at last / And turned the key upon her, fast'. The rhyming of 'last' and 'fast' serves to highlight the fact that they have locked her in against her will. The effect of her resistance to her husband's sexual advances is intimated at the end of the poem:

> She sleeps up in the attic there
> Alone, poor maid. 'Tis but a stair
> Betwixt us. Oh! my God! the down
> The soft young down of her, the brown,
> The brown of her – her eyes, her hair, her hair!

The use of the word 'maid', meaning virgin, suggests that the marriage has never been consummated. He calls her a 'poor maid' suggesting he feels sympathy and benevolence towards her; however, the last three lines demonstrate her subversion of his sexual power as it is he who seems to be reduced to lamenting their lack of contact.

Again on the subject of gender relations, Mew's short story 'Elinor' plays out the tensions for the 'New Woman' in the early twentieth century. Its protagonist is caught between a desire to write and her attraction towards a man. Her sister Jean, the narrator of the story, meditates on the nature of Elinor's dilemma:

> My thought took shape in her remembered words: 'The soul is bound with many chains – the cruellest, pride, the subtlest, suffering, and the deadliest, that which – men call love.' Her strength was failing by degrees, beneath this triple pressure.
>
> Love came simply to me; my heart went gladly out to meet it; but she confronted it (this much at least was plain to me) with desperate revolt.

It is as though Elinor envisages her own demise within the quotation her sister recounts, and indeed, at the end of the story, she dies. There is an element of piety in Jean's tone, and her choice of 'memory' to recount: Elinor has talked of 'pride,' 'suffering' and 'love', which are all feelings spoken of at length in the Bible, a touchstone in Mew's work. However, the inclusion of the first two emotions within the hyphens, and the third ('love') outside, suggests this is to be linked with the first clause of the sentence – 'the soul is bound with many chains' – giving it thematic prominence. Furthermore 'love' is presented as a bind in the use of the image of the 'chains', which implies entrapment, as well as being something men have perhaps created, or at least named: 'men call love.' Jean's pious tone, with almost an air of superiority, is more apparent at the latter end of her observations – 'Love came simply to me; my heart went gladly out to meet it' – signalling her role in the story as the 'traditional' woman to be contrasted with Elinor's behaviour in the last clause of the sentence: 'she confronted it [love]...with desperate revolt.' She is the 'New Woman,' struggling with traditional notions of femininity, as opposed to more modern ideals.

Mew's work blends many traditional characteristics with proto-modernist elements, and she is sometimes positioned on the bridge between Victorianism and modernism. Her wide thematic concerns in many ways speak well to the twenty-first century, covering marginalization, emancipation, sexuality, ecology and war.

WAR POETRY

The Great War directly influenced the literature produced in the years following it in a way that could not be said of the Second World War. Poetry and prose were changed, with the war acting as a catalyst for the incipient revolution in both literary form and content. In terms of the transformation of English poetry evident in the work of those who have come to be called the war poets, it is clear that the self-satisfied poetry of the recent past needed to be broken to cope with the brutal reality of the present. This is often seen as a development parallel to the revolution in poetry undertaken by Ezra Pound and others, and the war poets identified a new direction for British poetry that was not taken because so many of them died and their poems were slow in reaching publication.

Aside from an imagist like Richard Aldington, the impact of modernism was not strongly felt by the war poets in the trenches, but its formal and linguistic experimentations are explored in David Jones's prose-poem *In Parenthesis*, informed by his experiences as a private at the Battle of the Somme. Published in 1937, it is a lyrical meditation on a Welsh battalion's journey from training ground to battlefield:

> Dark-faceted iron oval lobs heavily to fungus-cushioned dank, wobbles under low leaf to lie, near where the heel drew out just now; and tough root-fibres boomerang to top-most green filigree and earth clods flung disturb fresh fragile shoots that brush the sky.

The single most striking fact of the Great War is still its scale in comparison with previous conflicts. In the Boer War, from 1899 to 1902, around 29,000 British soldiers died in the fighting and a further 16,000 from disease. By contrast, over eight and a half million soldiers died in the Great War and 20 million were wounded. The range of emotions stimulated by such events, combined with the new experiences at home, meant that more people were looking for ways to express their feelings; perhaps consequently, *The Times* reported receiving up to 100 poems a day in August 1915. On the one hand, most published poetry was written by officers, following the vogue for the Georgian verse of Rupert Brooke, especially after his death near the start of the war. On the other hand, *The Oxford Book of English Verse* was a common choice for a soldier's kitbag, and its study informed the work of many poets. Most of the now well-known protest writers, such as Wilfred Owen and Isaac Rosenberg, were not widely recognized or published until long after 1918, such that Philip Hobsbaum argued in 1961 that the most important missing pieces in English poetry in the twentieth century were the three poets killed in the war who had been developing an essentially English modernity: Owen, Thomas and Rosenberg.

Many critics would agree that Owen, Thomas and Rosenberg were the finest poets to be writing during the war. Along with Sassoon, Edmund Blunden, Ivor Gurney, Charles Sorley and Rupert Brooke, they are certainly the most discussed. Of these, only Rosenberg and Gurney were not officers. All were under 30, and all but Rosenberg are also included in James Reeves's 1962 anthology of *Georgian* poets. With very few exceptions, this is what the war poets were, but 'the Georgians' in poetry were not the rebellious figures that Virginia Woolf's 'Georgian' modernists were in prose – though they thought they were.

Owen's work only came to the fore in the 1930s, when poets interested in writing political verse, such as Auden and Spender, saw in him a precursor. Only four poems were published in his lifetime, and it was Edith Sitwell, in her pro-modernist *Wheels* magazine, who first brought him to public attention in 1919. Where a poet like Sassoon expresses indignation and bitterness, Owen appears more emotionally involved. He is neither satirical nor polemical, but his poems document the futility of war, the sense of waste. Rosenberg was a Jew of Lithuanian and Latvian origin, who attended the Slade Art School from 1911 to 1914 and joined the King's Own Royal Lancaster Regiment in 1915. The war arguably had little effect on his poetry in terms of style or tone, and it is likely that his class and ethnic background are more important influences. His poetry uses juxtaposed images, contrasting nature and warfare, to convey complexity and ambivalence, and, as might be expected of a painter, his poetry is very visual. Rosenberg described the war as 'A burnt space through ripe fields, / A fair mouth's broken tooth' ('August 1914') and envisioned the fighting in terms of mythic desires and doomed struggles. Rosenberg represented perhaps the most interesting poetry being written in the trenches and, along with Owen, he might have indicated a new direction for English poetry, but after the war the revolution in verse was continued by the American expatriates Pound and Eliot.

LATER CONRAD

Following on from his previous treatment of anarchists in England in *The Secret Agent*, Conrad's four-part spy-novel *Under Western Eyes* (1911) was informed by his early life in Russian-held Poland, his parents' radical political activities, and his education in Switzerland after his parents' death. It is a story concerned with revolutionaries in a Russian police-state under the Tsar, but the narrator is an Englishman who teaches languages in Geneva. His story is composed of his own observations combined with the diary of a Russian student called Kyrilo Sidorovitch Razumov, and he sees himself as 'a mute witness of things Russian, unrolling their Eastern logic under my Western eyes'.

Published first in serial form in *The English Review* six years before the Russian revolution, *Under Western Eyes* has an obvious prophetic appeal and is also a fascinating insight into a Tsarist Russia that was soon to disappear. The novel met with a strong critical, but poor commercial, success. Its reputation among Conrad's works has stayed high, and for several critics it is his last masterpiece, having much in common with the best of his other work. While the story is most like *The Secret Agent* in subject matter, *Under Western Eyes* is comparable to *Heart of Darkness*, in that it is told through the lens of a first-person narrator whose views are as important as the story he tells. It is additionally reminiscent of *Lord Jim*, in that it concerns a man who is guilty of betraying the confidence of others and who comes to seek redemption. It is also similar to the later novel *Victory*, in that it concerns a reclusive character, Razumov, who is forced by others to participate in a wider life, leading to his downfall. When asked to harbour a conspirator, Razumov betrays him and becomes a secret agent who infiltrates the executed man's group of revolutionary friends in Switzerland. Conrad's own conclusion on the book's significance occurs in his Author's Note, written in 1920:

> The most terrifying reflection ... is that all these people are not the product of the exceptional but of the general – of the normality of their place, and time, and race. The ferocity and imbecility of an autocratic rule rejecting all legality and in fact basing itself

upon complete moral anarchism provokes the no less imbecile and atrocious answer of a purely Utopian revolutionism encompass- ing destruction by the first means to hand, in the strange convic- tion that a fundamental change of hearts must follow the downfall of any given human institutions.

Conrad himself suffered a nervous breakdown when he finished the novel. He was wrapped up in the characters he had created, which were closer to his childhood than anything he had so far written, and oppressed by his continuing financial difficulties.

A glut of publications followed in 1912: the memoir sketches of *Some Reminiscences* (known as *A Personal Record* since its U.S. pub- lication), the tales of *'Twixt Land and Sea* (including 'The Secret Sharer', often considered his best short story), and the serialization of the work that brought him financial success and popular recogni- tion, *Chance: A Tale in Two Parts*, in the *New York Herald*. The rea- sons for *Chance*'s popularity, rather than any of Conrad's other novels, have been variously identified as its prestigious American serialization, the greater prominence given to women, publishers' publicity drives and even the book's cover. Born in Russian Poland, Conrad was enabled by the success of *Chance* and advances on his next novel to take his family for a nostalgic visit to his home country in 1914, a journey that nearly ended in internment when it was inter- rupted by the outbreak of World War I – a war whose end, after the Russian Revolution, would see established the new republic of the Polish State. After 1914 and up to his death ten years later, Conrad prospered, but the quality of much of his publications deteriorated, with the possible exception of two wartime works. One is the long story *The Shadow-Line* (1917), a tale which, like his early works, con- cerns an individual at a turning-point in his life. It was inspired by Conrad's thoughts of his eldest son, Borys, who had enlisted in the army. The other is the novel *Victory: An Island Tale* (1915), a narra- tive ostensibly concerning a failed trading company, sexual jealousy and multiple murder in Indonesia. It is a transitional novel, not often now considered alongside his earlier masterpieces, but superior to anything of comparable length that he wrote afterwards.

Set in Indonesia, *Victory* returned to the subject matter of Conrad's first books and was the kind of tropical island adventure story that Conrad knew Hollywood filmmakers would admire. First published in serial form in the London *Star*, the novel unfolds in four parts and is probably set in the 1890s. Its narrator, as is common in Conrad, is an anonymous character who speaks in the first person at times, especially at the beginning of the novel, but for most of the book relates the story as though he were an omniscient narrator.

With a plot in some ways reminiscent of *Lord Jim*, the main interest of the novel arguably lies in the paradox of the hero Axel Heyst's character: he is antisocial and hermitic, but at the same time he has a streak of the Samaritan in him, which outweighs his inclination to avoid socialization. This complexity, pitching rational pessimism against human feeling, is in contrast to the schematized portrayal of his antagonist Jones, who is described as both Satan incarnate and a wanderer-bandit shunned by polite English society for his misdemeanours. When he arrives at Heyst's bungalow, Jones announces 'I am the world itself, come to pay you a visit,' as though emphasizing that Heyst cannot escape society, however much he would like to live out his days in isolation. Jones therefore serves a function as an archetype, the death-bringer, amongst all the other archetypes within the narrative.

Victory has had a varied response from critics, some regarding it near Conrad's best, and others seeing it as deeply flawed. Detractors point to the sexual crudities and the unconvincing stock characters, such as Jones and the other villains, whose speech is often as overfamiliar as their type. Yet for other critics, the story has both the symbolic complexity and the narrative simplicity of a morality play. Heyst is arguably one of Conrad's most intriguing characters, and the story overall successfully dramatizes competing worldviews through the technique of shifting perspective from character to character. In terms of its critical reception, it remains Conrad's most controversial novel, but it does, in Leo Gurko's opinion in *Joseph Conrad: Giant in Exile* (1979), stand as 'a kind of one-volume summary of Conrad's collected works'.

SONS AND LOVERS (1913)

David Herbert Lawrence was born in the Nottinghamshire mining town of Eastwood on 11 September 1885. Educated in Nottingham, he became a teacher and then a full-time writer. His first publications were poems, which remain among his best work, and his first novel, *The White Peacock*, followed in 1911, the year he eloped with Frieda von Richtofen, who was married to a professor Lawrence had worked under at Nottingham University.

Lawrence is often most associated with challenging existing stereotypes of class and sexuality. He promoted feeling and full-living above tradition and conformity, advocating free thought and unfettered relationships that could be liberating rather than confining for the individual, and arguing that 'There is one clue to the universe. And that is the individual soul within the individual being'. Like much of his writing, his early novel *Sons and Lovers* was attacked by the censors. Not restored to its whole until 1992, the original publication was an expurgated and heavily edited one, plus it had already been rewritten several times from Lawrence's original conception of minimally fictionalized autobiography. The book considers love in its many forms, from parental to romantic, from love of writing to love of nature. Lawrence saw Victorian England in terms of its constrictions and denials, prescribing a life hemmed in by rules and duties, while proscribing a fuller, deeper life of intimacy and expression.

Sons and Lovers follows the struggles of a family of sons to transcend the love of their mother, a passionate woman of character who has married for love, but 'beneath herself', in the language of the time. All the sons fight with their father, who is positioned as a rival for their mother's love. In particular, it is the story of Paul Morel's endeavour to satisfy both his desire to please and his desire to rebel against suffocating social commandments to obey and conform. Like his elder brother William, Paul is devoted to his mother and forced to realize that he cannot break free from her love. Ultimately, it is she who has to relinquish her hold on him – a realization that precipitates her descent towards death.

Lawrence's own mother had died in 1910, and he had written about her as his 'first, great love'. He saw her as both the owner of his soul and the barrier to his self-fulfilment. Deeply devoted to her, he had even assisted her death by administering a dose of morphine. The Oedipal dimension to *Sons and Lovers* was recognized soon after its publication, and the novel's title expresses this directly, implying that the men whose lives it follows are both sons and lovers to their mother. While other literary examples abound, including *Hamlet*, Lawrence's *Sons and Lovers* is often held up as the exemplary early twentieth-century novel of mother-son relationships, finding a female companion piece in Katherine Mansfield's short story 'Daughters of the Late

Colonel'. Lawrence first met Mansfield in the year *Sons and Lovers* was published, and he and Frieda lived with Mansfield and John Middleton Murry during the war. The four of them were to be models for the central characters in Lawrence's later novel *Women in Love*.

Like the novels of Hardy, a writer whose example was crucial for Lawrence in working through his own ideas in his seminal *Study of Thomas Hardy*, Lawrence's work charts the changes wrought on the land and the people by the coming of industrialization. This is evident from the first page of *Sons and Lovers*: 'Then, some sixty years ago, a sudden change took place. The gin-pits were elbowed aside by the large mines of the financiers. The coal and iron field of Nottinghamshire and Derbyshire was discovered. Carston, Waite and Co. appeared. Amid tremendous excitement, Lord Palmerston formally opened the company's first mine at Spinney Park, on the edge of Sherwood Forest' (Lawrence 1956: 5). From this forceful opening of lives violently transformed, Lawrence goes on to draw in detail the violent emotions and frustrations of adolescence, sexual awakening, competing loves and cultural class struggle. As a foundational story of twentieth-century working-class life, it sits at the more experimental, personal end of the spectrum, at the other end of a line of proletarian fiction from the socialist politics of Robert Tressell's equally important, but formally more conservative, *The Ragged Trousered Philanthropists*, published the following year.

Whether or not Lawrence is best considered a modernist is a contentious point. He is in many ways a radical writer, but for several critics he takes existing fictional styles in new directions, his revolution of the novel subsisting more at the level of character and motivation than form and language. His narrative voice rests on top of all his fiction, and there is little aesthetic innovation, meaning that the traditional hierarchies of discourse in Austen, Dickens or Eliot are still present. However, in his use of myth, consciousness and dynamic interpersonal relationships, Lawrence is more of a modernist than he is an Edwardian or a realist. Which is to say that he is in many ways a one-off: all writers may claim to be unique, but few present as great a problem for the categorizations of literary history as Lawrence. *Sons and Lovers* was also in many ways an apprentice work, whose style would be radically evolved in Lawrence's later writings, which are more frequently considered modernist, *The Rainbow* and, particularly, *Women in Love*.

THE RAINBOW (1915)

On publication of *The Rainbow*, Lawrence was prosecuted for using profane language and writing frankly about sex. The novel was suppressed, and many hundreds of copies burned. His aim in the book, however, is far more rounded and complex than his detractors appreciated. Lawrence portrays individuals driven by unconscious impulses and divided within themselves. Consistent characters are thus forsaken for wilful, pluralistic spirits that reflect the diversity of human experience, opposed, for example, to the largely static personalities attributed to figures in the fiction of Dickens.

The Rainbow spans several generations of the Brangwen family and chronicles the breakdown of a social order over many decades. Drawing on both theistic and pantheistic imagery, Lawrence lends a mythic and epic grandeur to his depiction of lives rooted in the English land transformed by the juggernaut of historical change and the force of individual passions. It is life, rather than art, that drives Lawrence's writing, and here lies his distinction from Ezra Pound, James Joyce and Wyndham Lewis. Lawrence believed in organic form rather than *bons mots*, and he found too many experimental writers around him to be followers of French theory and the aesthetics of Flaubertian impersonality, so distant from his own emphasis on engaged living. Partly influenced by Italian futurism, Lawrence wished to show that humans were part of the universe, and the forces that drove them were natural, rather than civilized. This is partly evident in the repetitions, which Lawrence saw as rhythms, that pulse though his writing, informing a new language that expressed, more than described, a life force.

The passions of their lives are shown in the characters' occupations, from Will Brangwen's woodcarving and care for the soil through to Ursula's interest in education and teaching. The land roots them in their natural existence, while history careers about them. The Brangwens remain tied to elemental forces derived from the land and their farming heritage, but social forces take their lives in new directions: enfranchisement, mass education, industrialization, new transport systems, colonialism and war.

A highly symbolic work, *The Rainbow* is the first of Lawrence's novels to show his deep interest in myth and the visionary alongside the development of modern character as the generations of the

Brangwen family issue in the modern woman, Ursula. Ursula is a distinct and self-fashioning character in the third generation of the Brangwen family treated in the story: she breaks free from the stream of life that Lawrence associates with wave, river and flood imagery to encounter a rebirth or germination of self at the moment she loses her unborn child. The novel ends with the image of the rainbow emerging over the new estates, representing her transformation, but also a ray of bright hope over the future.

In his vital essay 'Morality and the Novel', Lawrence writes a sentence which partly explains the symbol in the title of his novel: 'The novel is the perfect medium for revealing to us the changing rainbow of our living relationships'. It is the importance of relationships and relatedness to 'life' that Lawrence avers in this essay and which forms his argument for why the novel is morally important as 'the highest example of subtle inter-relatedness that man has discovered' (Lawrence 1971: 177). The essay begins by asserting that the purpose of art is to uncover humans' connection with the universe, and goes on to say that ' life consists in this achievement of a pure relationship between ourselves and the living universe'. (Lawrence 1971: 176) Lawrence asserts that people can never know what reality is, but can reveal the relation they have with nature and reality. And for Lawrence, morality is truth to life and to its interrelatedness: 'The only morality is to have man true to his manhood, woman to her womanhood, and let the relationship form of itself, in all honour. For it is, to each, life itself'. *The Rainbow* expresses this forcefully, but it would be several years before Ursula's continued story reached publication in *Women in Love*, a book with a new style that showed Lawrence's writing evolving alongside the war years and the experiments of the modernist writers around him.

DUBLINERS (1914)

A collection of 15 stories that amount to a story cycle and move from childhood through to maturity, *Dubliners* portrays the capital of Ireland, second city of the British Empire, as the heart of paralysis. The stories depict aspects to the stultifying atmosphere of the city that Stephen Dedalus will try to escape in Joyce's first novel, discussed in the next section. Paralysis is shown in the characters' inability to move beyond their circumstances, but also in the symbolism deployed throughout the stories, where decay, dust, death, corruption, frustration and darkness abound.

The stories may be considered in five sections: childhood, adolescence, maturity, public life and death. The first three stories centre on encounters between children and the adult world, in which the young are exposed to the corruptions of elders in terms of the influence of the Church, predatory sexuality and commerce. The division between experience and innocence is drawn as one between exploiters and the exploited, whose youthful hopes appear frustrated by a cynical adult world. Some recent analysis has been concerned with Joyce's position in terms of imperialism and first- and third-world divisions. This has often concentrated on the Irish as colonized Europeans, as imperial insiders and outsiders. The frustration and ambivalence of such a position is present at the end of the third story 'Araby', in which a romantic young Dubliner finds his reverential dream of the almost-sacred Oriental bazaar brought down to earth by the taint of economic and linguistic colonial corruption he senses before the English stallholders at the Royal Dublin Society show grounds.

The second group of stories considers young adulthood and is focused on issues of romance and marriage, money and sex. The first and last of the four stories consider two unsuitable marriages; the first portrays 'Eveline' as a woman tempted but immobilized by Frank's promise of escape to South America, while 'The Boarding House' has Bob Doran (aged 35) and Polly Mooney (aged 19) trapped in an engagement unsuitable for both of them, but engineered by Polly's upwardly mobile mother, who is also Bob's landlady, Mrs Mooney.

The four stories of maturity portray frustrations and disconnections in later life. 'A Little Cloud' depicts a man's personal and professional failure as he realizes that his life has passed him by and others have taken centre stage; 'Counterparts' centres on an alcoholic father who takes home his frustrations; and 'Clay' follows an old maid returning to the family of her foster child for a Halloween party. The fourth story, 'A Painful Case' most poignantly underlines the consequences of inaction and frustration in middle age as a man discovers that his decision not to marry a woman four years earlier has precipitated a descent in her psychological well-being that has led to her death, as reported in his newspaper.

Politics, family and religion are the themes for the stories of public life. 'Ivy Day in the Committee Room' has a missing centre of the politician Charles Stewart Parnell. Parnell was Joyce's political hero, and with Michael Davitt he had founded the important Irish political campaign group the Land League in 1879. He then became leader of 61 Home Rule League members elected to Parliament in 1880, and he pressed unceasingly for Irish Independence over the following decade. In the story, Joyce vents his feelings about the political disarray following the denunciation of Parnell by the Church and his own bitter feelings about Parnell's betrayal by the priests and by their followers in Ireland. 'A Mother' tells a story of a woman who puts her daughter to the fore in a series of musical concerts to compensate, unsuccessfully, for her own young frustrated romantic desires after she has married a much older man 'out of spite' at her other suitors. 'Grace' depicts the attempts to transform and reform a drunken man through Catholicism.

Most significant in the collection is the final and longest story of the volume, 'The Dead'. It focuses on the Morkan sisters' twelfth night party and, in particular, the invited couple Gabriel and Gretta Conroy. The story culminates in the Gresham hotel as the couple prepare for bed. Here we find Gabriel staring out of their bedroom window at the shroud of snow that is falling over all Ireland, after hearing that the love of his wife's life was a passionate boy from the West Coast of Ireland called Michael Furey, now long dead. Gabriel imagines himself looking out on the lifeless streets, in contrast to Gretta looking out from her bedroom window in Galway at the brave but consumptive boy from the gasworks, Michael, a spiritual counterpart to Parnell's political force when Gretta was a girl. Gabriel is solid and dependable, but unexciting and unromantic, in contrast to the fervour and fragility associated with the Celtic Renaissance far away from Dublin. Gabriel experiences a 'vague terror' and is transfixed at the end in a spiritual torpor symbolizing once more the paralysis Joyce castigated in Ireland's politics, religion, culture and colonial status.

Dubliners indicates Joyce's later fully modernist style in its emphasis on symbolism and the plasticity of language. There is less linguistic play than in his subsequent work, but the stories show him honing a style indebted to Chekhov and Flaubert as well as ideas derived from diverse writers such as Walter Pater and Thomas Aquinas.

A PORTRAIT OF THE ARTIST AS A YOUNG MAN (1916)

A Portrait is, in essence, the semi-autobiographical story of the development of a young man from infancy to the end of his teens, over the years 1883 to 1903. It is a rewritten version of *Stephen Hero*, a long Edwardian novel that Joyce abandoned to fashion into five long epiphanic chapters. In his youth, Joyce wrote epiphanies, similar to prose poems, as an artistic exercise. He took the term from the Bible, where it refers to a divine revelation, such as the manifestation of Christ to the Magi. For Joyce, however, an epiphany was the 'revelation of the whatness of the thing', the point at which 'the soul of the commonest object ... seems to us radiant' as he explained in *Stephen Hero*. He felt there was an obligation on the artist to discover a spiritual truth in everyday life, and, after the anti-epiphanies of the paralysed protagonists in *Dubliners*, in *A Portrait of the Artist as a Young Man* each epiphany for Stephen at the close of the first four parts is a synthesis of triumph which the next chapter destroys.

First serialized from February 1914 to September 1915, and sometimes considered the first fully modernist Anglophone prose work, Joyce's novel moves through a series of searches for self: attempts to 'forge' an identity and free the protagonist's soul. It ends in dispersal as Stephen Dedalus's journal entries dissolve the book into fragments. In these last pages Stephen is 'portrayed' as a cubistic collage of miscellaneous impulses and consciousnesses. This is just before his departure from Dublin, with Stephen effecting the escape that froze all the central characters in *Dubliners*. In his role as Icarus (the son of Daedalus in Greek mythology), Stephen is poised to take the flight that he thinks will free him from the chains of religion and family in Ireland. It is considered to be an assertion of individual will on the part of the artist, as Stephen proclaims his self-origin and the forging of his own racial conscience, of the 'race' that he has come from, that has produced him.

The fractured, ungrammatical language at the end of the novel also echoes that used at the beginning, when Stephen comes to an awareness of his sense impressions mediating the world around him. The syntax in this first section of the novel is simple, the opening page for example comprising full-stops and colons, rather than a range of punctuation; the only commas are present in songs and in the speech of adults. It is also worth mentioning that Joyce uses dashes and not quotation marks to indicate speech, because he wants the words to appear as a part of the narrative, and quotation marks would isolate them.

Utilizing in *A Portrait* a style that would be adapted by other modernists, such as Woolf and Mansfield, the narrative takes on the manner of the characters without actually using first person narration or transcribing their speech or thoughts. It is chiefly focused through the camera eye of Stephen's consciousness, but also at any point employs the language of the character being described by the narrator (Wyndham Lewis famously criticized Joyce for observing that a character 'repaired' to the outhouse, using a hackneyed expression, but Joyce's defenders reply that this is the word that the character, Stephen's Uncle Charles, would have used).

As noted above, each chapter ends with a triumph, which the next destroys. The first covers early childhood, family and Stephen's removal to a Jesuitical school at Clongowes in County Kildare. The second centres on his adolescence at Belvedere College in Dublin, his burgeoning erotic imagination, and his time spent acting, defending his literary and philosophical heroes, and finally fantasizing about sex, all of which culminates in a humiliating visit to a prostitute. The theme of the third chapter is 'sin' and religion; the opening plays on the seven deadly sins (gluttony, lust, sloth, pride, wrath, avarice, envy) and a long kinetic sermon about hell at a retreat, ending in Stephen's confession. The fourth part sees the rise of art to the forefront of Stephen's mind and his decision to go to University and not enter the Church. It ends in a lyrical passage in which Stephen swoons as he watches a girl on the beach, who he envisages as a bird who inspires his soul. The fifth and final chapter focuses on Stephen's time at University and the synthesis of his thought in an aesthetic philosophy, derived from Aquinas.

A Portrait has many symbols, but the fundamental one is of a creature trying to break away from the bondage of the grosser elements of life in Ireland, dominated by British Rule and Roman Catholicism, and learn to fly. The story concludes with Stephen intending to flee the nets of religion, family and nation: 'I will not serve that in which I no longer believe, whether it call itself my home, my fatherland, or my church: and I will try to express myself in some mode of life or art as freely as I can and as wholly as I can, using for my defence the only arms I allow myself to use – silence, exile, and cunning.' (Joyce 1960: 247) Stephen's assertion 'I will not serve', which was also Lucifer's, is made to emphasize Stephen's defiance of authority, but the next time we encounter him is in 1904, still in Dublin, at the start of *Ulysses*.

THE GOOD SOLDIER (1915)

Ford Madox Ford's novel is told by John Dowell, a rich Philadelphian Quaker who has no occupation. He recounts the events of his life in an effort to understand what has happened to him and to those around him. The people he is principally interested in are his dead wife, Florence, and his close friends Edward and Leonora Ashburnham. The four of them seem to have been happy, moneyed couples. They have had every opportunity in life and see their principal task in society to be setting a good 'standard'. The novel explores the surface conventions and the private passions and hypocrisies of these putative models of social behaviour. The most significant event of the first half of the novel is the affair between Florence and Edward. The major issue of the second half is the relationship between Edward and a young woman, Nancy Rufford, who is the Ashburnhams' ward. *The Good Soldier* is subtitled 'A Tale of 'Passion' and it could be described as a narrative based around the infidelities of its discredited hero, Edward Ashburnham. The novel is narrated over two years in all. Dowell writes initially for half a year, then there is an 18-month gap.

An Old World is presented in the novel as the upper-class, leisured, conventional Edwardian society which tries to perpetuate Victorian moral standards and propriety. The characters have empty lives with no employment, no family and no purpose. Above all, with these characters it is the public facade that counts: Dowell says they have a dread of 'scenes, scandals, publicity, or open confrontations'. 'The Good Soldier' was not Ford's desired title for the book, but if we take it ironically it has some relevance. Dowell says at one point that good soldiers found their profession 'full of big words, courage, loyalty, honour, constancy.' The novel suggests that in the twentieth century these are all just words; in the book, Ashburnham has even ceased being a soldier when Dowell meets him. Writing at the start of the War, Ford is able to suggest the falsity of these grand labels, anticipating the poetry of soldiers like Sassoon, who helped to discredit them by the end of the war. Ford presents a social group whose class manufactured the war, but who remain ignorant of it; their idle wasted lives hint at the pointless devastation to come.

The novel's epigraph on its title page is '*Beati Immaculati*'. The complete line from Matthew's Gospel is translated as "Blessed are the pure; for they shall see God.' This is yet another of the novel's ironies, as none of the four main protagonists approaches purity, and the only person who turns to face God is Nancy, who has been driven insane by the others' duplicity and insincerity. So, we are given a respectable, admired class of people who have mislaid their sense of responsibility and social commitment. The old world is also important in respect of the war. Ford began writing the novel in December 1913, and by the time it was published in 1915 he was a soldier himself. The Edwardian world before the Great War is frequently pictured as a world of illusion: rationalism and scientific endeavour still seemed to be the saviours of the Western World, and 'civilization' was considered to be on a march of confident progress. The First World War shattered this, revealing the arrogance of the Western powers and that science was in fact to be used to kill and destroy – another unmasking of conventional wisdom. One of Ford's principal criticisms of the idle classes is their ignorance of or indifference to the approaching war. Setting the novel for the most part in Germany seemed also to be a criticism of the current conflict, especially considering that Ford was of German extraction (his real name being Hueffer, the name under which the novel appeared when first serialized).

The old world is ultimately summed up by the epithet 'good people', referring to the veneer of accepted conventional manners that signal breeding and money. Dowell says: 'The queer thing is that the whole collection of rules applies to anybody – to the anybodies that you meet in hotels, in railway stations... upon steamers. You meet a man or a women and, from tiny and intimate sounds, from the slightest of movements, you know at once whether you are concerned with good people or with those who won't do.' Dowell's belief in propriety continues to the end of the novel where, in the last sentences, he neither prevents Ashburnham's suicide nor speaks to him because, he says, it would not be 'English good form'. Dowell's conclusion on the old order persisting into the modern world is brief: he says, 'I think that it would have been better in the eyes of God if they had all attempted to gouge out each other's eyes with carving knives. But they were "good people".'

In terms of its status as a modernist text, the novel uses a peculiar time scheme, and, moving between past and present in this way, it is unlike almost any nineteenth-century English novel except *Wuthering Heights*. In terms of space, it also moves from location to location – Nauheim, the cruise ship, the country house, and so forth. There is no point of stability, and travelling from place to place is as common as staying in one locality. The characters are consequently represented as adrift, or homeless. Dowell says at one point, 'We are almost always in one place with our mind's somewhere quite other.' Modernism is noted for shifting emphases from the external world to the internal, and in Ford's story Dowell's perceptions do not simply mediate the story; they are the story.

The narrative is also fragmented, not least because the story is told piecemeal. There is no attempt to tell the tale chronologically or in accordance with any other principle of order. It is told through memories, and so is arranged by association and reflection. It is also solipsistic and introverted; not a social novel in the nineteenth-century manner. Few scenes last more than one page; it is disjointed, and dialogue is minimal; Dowell rarely quotes more than two sentences. This is one aspect in which modernism is arguably more realistic than realism. There is, additionally, no attempt to create traditional narrative suspense and tension. Early on, Dowell exposes events that are going to happen later in the story, such as Florence's death, as though these were trivial details. Lastly, the narrator, Dowell, is unsure and confused, full of doubt and self-doubt, like Marlow in Conrad's *Heart of Darkness*.

Ford wrote the novel thinking it might be his last, and he wanted it to be a transitional text from the Edwardian realists to the aesthetics of new writers like Pound and Eliot.

IN A GERMAN PENSION (1911) AND *BLISS* (1920)

Born in 1888, Katherine Mansfield came permanently to Europe from New Zealand in 1908, after a previous period as a music student in London. She is associated almost exclusively with the short story, which she developed in the lyrical style of Chekhov, rather than in pursuit of the well-made tale of Maupassant, Stevenson and Hawthorne. Her first collection, *In a German Pension*, followed on from a stay in Bavaria, where she went to avoid scandal over a pregnancy, but which resulted in a miscarriage. She achieved success with *Bliss and Other Stories*, a noticeably more accomplished collection.

Mansfield's first collection has stories that contain fine writing, but also passages that seem callow or trenchant, aggressive or embattled. There is a sense that she is not yet fully comfortable with her own voice and prose. This changes with the second volume and is noticeable from the opening three stories. She worked on the first, 'Prelude', from 1915 to 1917, and the story was first published by the Woolfs through their Hogarth Press. In the process of shaping this new kind of work, after three years in which she wrote almost nothing, Mansfield developed her mature style and method through a long, reflective and lyrical story of her childhood in New Zealand. Over the course of 12 parts, first envisaged as the start of a novel, 'Prelude' consistently and convincingly conveys the impressions drawn by the characters in the story without moving away from the third person. The narrative presence is almost expunged by a technique that conveys events as though filtered though the emotional prism of the shared unconscious of the family at the heart of this elegiac paean to Mansfield's island home. Set initially on the day of a house move, it is a story of change and disruption, suggesting the nostalgic approach to a lost past, but it is also a very modern tale in exposing the fears of individuals and the group discordances at the dysfunctional core of a happy family. In the first advanced short story of modernist psychological realism that she would perfect, Mansfield's narration and symbolism expose the underbelly of the characters' thoughts, and move the reader into a vantage point from which to view the tensions apparent in three generations of a family, emerging from which is a young girl, Kezia, anticipating Laura in Mansfield's best-known story, 'The Garden Party', who begins to imagine things in terms other than those of the traditions she has inherited.

The following two stories were written early in 1918, after Mansfield finished 'Prelude'. They are well-crafted and intriguing analyses of sexual ethics and interplay. The first, '*Je ne parle pas francais*', again marks Mansfield's new confidence as she focuses the entire story through the main character, whose perspective has to be seen beyond by the reader. A monologue on the past from someone who claims never to look back, it is at heart a sad narrative of failed love in a callous world. Told as though in conversation by a man seated in a Parisian cafe, it is a story that can also be read in many ways. Its narrator, Duquette, is an artist of high intelligence by his own judgment, but his described behaviour would also suggest a high degree of moral flexibility, as he seeks to manipulate the couple at the heart of the story, Dick Harmon and his lover, Mouse. Duquette toys with each of them and considers that he might exploit them to further his interest in the sexual underworld of his society. However, Harmon proves to be more committed to his mother than to Mouse, who is the prey of the men in the story. Naively innocent, she is abandoned and unable to speak the language, literally and metaphorically, of the sophisticated people around her. Yet she causes Duquette to break his rule of not looking back, and this is a typical Mansfield ending, open to suggestions that it is guilt, missed opportunity, or pride that causes him to reflect.

'Bliss' is one of Mansfield's masterpieces. Another ambiguous and complex study of male-female relationships, it is a seemingly simple story. The central character, Bertha, is turning 30 and suffused with feelings of bliss on the day of a dinner party she is to give at her house. These feelings are associated with a childhood joy that Bertha has not translated into adult passions. She is constantly looking for a source of this exuberance, which may be in her home, her child, her husband, or herself. The party in the evening gives Mansfield the opportunity for some acute social satire of London pretensions, but Bertha comes to locate her happiness on one of her guests, Pearl Fulton. The story abounds with symbolism – the suggestive, appetizing fruit; the enclosed domestic garden; the wild moon; the phallic pear tree – but ends with the realization, for Bertha, that in wondering about the source of her well-being, she missed a stronger participation in life. The attractiveness she sees in Pearl has also been noticed by her husband, with whom Pearl is having an affair.

Mansfield was unimpressed by the suffragette movement, but there is arguably a good deal of feminist conviction underlying the perspective taken in several of her stories. Many of them depict women superficially like Mansfield, but who have stayed in the confines of their class and upbringing while yearning to break away.

The modernist short story, exemplified in the stories of Woolf and Mansfield, is not founded on unity, but on ambiguity and paradox. There can frequently be a tension between the control of the form/structure and the ambiguity of the content/meaning. They are studies of character or of 'moments', often with little conventional 'plot' but notable for suggestive, poetic and elliptical passages.

IMAGISM AND 'THE LOVE SONG OF
J. ALFRED PRUFROCK' (1917)

Imagism was one of many artistic movements that came to be grouped under the umbrella term of modernism, and it has been argued that it was the only one of these to greatly influence English poetry. The Georgian and war poet Edward Thomas was disapproving of imagists, considering them translators, paraphrasers, and even, as he wrote to one friend, 'imbeciles'. However, much Anglo-American prewar poetry has a poor reputation, because the work of Ezra Pound and other imagists and modernists was permanently to change the form and subject matter of English literature at the same time that the war poets were forging changes in diction and sentiment.

The creed of imagism has been expressed in polemical and prescriptive documents, but the poets' emphasis was always on precise and concrete presentation, without excess wordage. They disliked the iamb and abstractions, but favoured free verse, accuracy, directness and scientific principles in poetry. The idea of the 'image', influenced by the Japanese haiku and tanka as well as French symbolist poetry, summed up their preference for concision and compression. As Pound wrote in his *Memoir* of 1916: 'The image...is a radiant node or cluster; it is...a VORTEX, from which, and through which, and into which, ideas are constantly rushing' (Smith 1983: 3). Richard Aldington, one of the few British imagists, illustrates their principles in his poem 'Sunsets', of the same year:

> The white body of the evening
> Is torn into scarlet,
> Slashed and gouged and seared
> Into crimson,
> And hung ironically
> With garland of mist.
> And the wind
> Blowing over London from Flanders
> Has a bitter taste.

This is also a war poem, but not of the kind usually grouped under that name. It additionally reminds the reader of the opening to T. S. Eliot's most famous early poem 'The Love Song of J. Alfred

Prufrock' from *Prufrock and Other Observations* (1917): 'Let us go then, you and I, / When the evening is spread out against the sky / Like a patient etherized upon a table'.

In both criticism and poetry, Eliot sought discipline and structure. He disliked the tradition in art that promoted expressions of emotion and spontaneity, believing instead in a formulaic set of objects, events, or situations that evokes a particular emotion; he famously called this 'finding an objective correlative' in his essay 'Hamlet and His Problems' (1919). 'The Love Song of J. Alfred Prufrock' describes shifting patterns of thoughts and conceptions connected by inference or obscure principles of association that work beneath consciousness. Prufrock's memory selects images from both literature and experience, such that a model of the mind's organization is implied in the web of the poem, which, like the mind, weaves together perceptions, memories and cultural artefacts, forming them into new meanings. Prufrock himself is repeatedly unable to find the right words or express himself satisfactorily; even the prissy, formal title hints at Prufrock's insecurity and the sense of a life measured out in coffee spoons.

Prufrock's introspective preoccupation with himself is also representative of modernism. He fantasizes about various aliases or possibilities that never quite bring truth or happiness. In this way, the poem illustrates how a crisis over the self in modernist literature is also a crisis of language. In Prufrock's search for himself, Eliot's poem repeatedly problematizes the subject in relation to discourse. In his song, Prufrock is regrettably all too aware of the inadequacies of language: 'It is impossible to say just what I mean', he declares, and his desire to identify himself through language seems to fail like his attempt to position himself romantically or socially. Prufrock's sense of himself is highly dependent on 'The eyes that fix you in a formulated phrase' resulting in little internal self-confidence and little affirmation of his fitness as a lover.

Emphasizing the mythopoeic dimension of modernist reference, Prufrock's anxieties conjure up heroes from the past, but they also seem to represent his vacillation and procrastination. His alter egos, Lazarus and Hamlet, both fail to act and to say exactly what they mean. It is as though Prufrock is not the only one needing a love song; as we will find in Eliot's later *The Waste Land*, there are doubts as to whether modern life is amenable to the sentiment and formality implied by his attempted paean to love.

The pronouns in the poem move from 'I' to 'we' to 'us' suggesting both dispersal in the crowd and a shift from subject to object. In such ways, Prufrock appears an exemplary fragmented modernist self, caught in neuroses and doubts. Undermined by hidden desires, driven by the unconscious, lost in language, painfully self-conscious and detached, Prufrock seems to be one of the first modernist subjects in Anglo-American poetry.

TARR (1918)

A painter and writer, Wyndham Lewis moved to Paris in 1902, after studying at the Slade School of Art, and travelled the European Continent for much of the remainder of the decade. He returned to London and his first stories were published in the *English Review* in 1909. In the following years he exhibited paintings with the Camden Town Group and launched his first and most influential magazine, *BLAST*. Though only published in two editions, one in 1914 and one the following year, *BLAST* has come to be seen as the clarion call of English modernism, indebted to, but soon divergent from, the futurist preachings of the Italian Filippo Tommaso Marinetti, who had visited England on a London lecture tour in 1910. The first edition of *BLAST*, in a lurid pink cover, contained Lewis's 20-page vorticist manifesto; contributions from Ezra Pound, Henri Gaudier-Brzeska, Jacob Epstein and Rebecca West; and an excerpt from *The Saddest Story*, which was to become Ford Madox Ford's novel *The Good Soldier*. Lewis also took the opportunity to either 'Blast' or 'Bless' contemporary artists, lambasting Roger Fry and the Bloomsbury set in particular. The second 'War' edition featured early poems by T. S. Eliot, including 'Rhapsody on a Windy Night', and again employed the striking typographical approach Lewis had derived and adapted from Marinetti.

Though he went on to become familiar with most of the major modernists, Lewis associated with Ezra Pound, Ford and T. S. Eliot at this time, and also began work on his first published novel, *Tarr*. This novel was based on his Parisian experiences as an artist and was serialized in *The Egoist* in 1916 and 1917. Influenced by Nietzsche, the book introduced Lewis as a polemical satirist of modern civilization and artistic Bohemia. He had read the modern Russian writers, such as Dostoevsky, in French translation in Paris and attended Henri Bergson's lectures at the College de France as well as become familiar with the work of painters such as Picasso, Derain and Modigliani. *Tarr* developed from a theatrical poem Lewis had written called *Enemy of the Stars*, possibly the first attempt at what would now be thought of as an English modernist prose work. Set in Montmartre, *Tarr* concentrates on a group of Bohemian artists and portrays them in vivid characterizations that are opposite to the interior monologues of Joyce and Woolf. In particular, the novel focuses on an Englishman, Tarr, modelled on Lewis, and a German romantic called Kreisler, detailing their struggles with money, sex and society. Tarr's Nietzschean postures include a rejection of the English sense of humour, which he thinks people use to avoid reality, and a condescending attitude to the rest of the middle-class Bohemians around him, whom he perceives to be inferior to his position as artistic superman.

A bridge between the underground world of Dostoevsky and the Nietzschean aesthetics of the Third Reich, Lewis's disdain for bourgeois life led him to be an early admirer of fascism. Sometimes thought to anticipate this extreme and violent right-wing stance, *Tarr* was first written in the years 1909 to 1911 and revised during the war, though its book publication date is 1918. A revised and in some ways more reader-friendly version of the novel was overseen by Lewis for publication by Chatto ten years later, three years before Lewis's study of the 'peace-lover' *Hitler* (1931), a perspective revoked in his later work *The Hitler Cult* (1939).

Lewis's reputation hangs on a variety of art forms, and he is one of the many polymaths who spurred Anglophone modernism on. The most avant-garde and cosmopolitan of contemporary 'English' writers (though he travelled extensively, his father was American, and he was born in Canada) his works are little read outside of academia, and he is best known for his vorticist experiments in painting during the Great War, combining futurism and cubism, and his vivid portraits of literary figures such as Eliot, Pound and Edith Sitwell. Of his other fictional prose works, probably the most read is *The Apes of God* (1930), another attack on London painters and intellectuals such as the Sitwells and the Bloomsbury group, but his critical studies remain important, including the monumental *Time and Western Man* (1927), an attack on the neglect of spatial aesthetics for overdetermining temporal theories in contemporary philosophy and art, typified by Bergson and Joyce.

PILGRIMAGE (1915–1953)

Dorothy Richardson's *Pilgrimage* is a 13-chapter sequence that began in 1913 with *Pointed Roofs*. The sequence of volumes, in which each 'chapter' is the length of a novel, is an almost Proustian search for identity in its scrutiny of a sensitive and intelligent young woman whose appetite for living is frustrated by her circumstances, but who finds solace in friends and deep reflection in the peaceful solitude of the private space of her room. *Pilgrimage*, in its early volumes, also offers an examination of the public space for a woman in late Victorian and Edwardian England.

Richardson rejects traditional emphases on character or plot and opts instead for an intense presentation from her protagonist Miriam's point of view. Richardson's critical work also pioneers aspects of the representation of women's reality in 'Women and the Future' (1924) and 'About Punctuation' (1924) through to her foreword for the first collected *Pilgrimage* in 1938. For recent feminist critics, these writings underline the politics and aesthetics of *Pilgrimage*'s long revisioning of the masculinist novel within both realism and modernism. *Pilgrimage* thus begins in the style of a new feminine realism, not formally radical or particularly innovative, except in terms of subject matter: an autobiographical self-scrutiny in fiction. However, Richardson is still reaching, in *Pointed Roofs*, towards an expressive and contemplative vision of reality influenced by the late work of Henry James (and the mentorship of H. G. Wells) and his technique, discussed earlier with regard to *The Wings of the Dove* and *The Ambassadors* in Chapter One, of focalizing the narrative through the limited point of view of one character's consciousness, rather than an omniscient narrator.

This approach of unfolding the narrative through Miriam's consciousness means that the usual novelistic descriptions and contextualizations for the benefit of the reader are largely absent, and it is perception and thought rather than third-person narration that drive the novels. This approach led Richardson to the composition of long stretches of text unbroken by paragraphs and also to increasing experimentation with punctuation, syntax and even layout. Because the text follows the form of thought, it often leaves out periods or dissolves in ellipsis and irresolution, with abrupt shifts between past and present and speech framed by Miriam's consciousness. In this, Richardson was deeply influenced by the work of Henri

Bergson, which both linked and distanced her from the work of other writers, such as Woolf and Mansfield, who focused considerably on character. By contrast, Richardson followed the dictates of her project's emphasis on thought unresolved by the self's social, temporal and spatial reordering of mental reality.

Pilgrimage is also an extended *Künstlerroman*, a novel about the development of an artist. The sense of a holy journey towards becoming a writer suggests the importance that Miriam Henderson places on language, particularly the unspoken language of the mind and of literature. She achieves her vocational aim in the unfinished final volume, *March Moonlight*, becoming a writer after many years of apprenticeship as a thoughtful, studious reader. For many critics, it is significant that Miriam comes to appreciate the complex relationship between writing, reading and gender, as well as sometimes between male and female criticism.

Richardson lived most of her adult life in London. She married a Bohemian artist in 1917 and moved in avant-garde circles such as the Bloomsbury group. She first published translations and freelance journalism, before eventually giving up regular secretarial work to become a full-time writer. In *Pilgrimage*, London, too, is perceived in gender terms that reflect the openness that Richardson found there. Whereas the male writers of the modernist era often understood urbanization as a negative development, Richardson saw the capital quite differently, as a labyrinthine metropolis that provided degrees of freedom and anonymity. The reader enters into this maze with Miriam, who is both guide and chaperone:

> Miriam left the gaslit hall and went slowly upstairs. The March twilight lay upon the landings, but the staircase was almost dark. The top landing was quite dark and silent. There was no one about. It would be quiet in her room. She could sit by the fire and be quiet and think things over until Eve and Harriet came back with the parcels. She would have time to think about the journey and decide what she was going to say to the Fräulein. (Richardson: 3)

This is the opening to *Pointed Roofs* and gives a sense of the reader's closeness to Miriam. That the narrative point of view originates from within Miriam's own consciousness is clear from phrases such as 'The March twilight lay upon the landings, but the staircase was almost dark. The top landing was quite dark and silent.' It is as though the reader is climbing the stairs with Miriam, seeing the 'March twilight' filtering onto the landings through what must be windows, then the climb of the 'almost dark' staircase. The sentence, 'There was no one about', gives the impression that Miriam is looking around her for others who might disrupt her solitude, emphasized by the repetition of the phrase 'be quiet' in the next lines. The last sentence again represents Miriam's thoughts flowing from those concerning her sisters, a temporal reflection, to thoughts of the future. This conclusion to the first paragraph of the book introduces the idea of 'the journey' or voyage, with the implication that Miriam is to travel abroad in her use of the German word 'Fräulein.' There is a sense of nervous anticipation about this meeting: she feels she has to 'decide what she was going to say'. Although we do not know at this stage that she is to become a governess, it is the adventure on which Miriam will start her quest to find her vocation as a writer.

MAY SINCLAIR

A noted and successful writer from the late nineteenth century to the 1930s, Sinclair became interested before the Great War in Freudian theory through the Medico-Psychological Clinic in London. She introduced psychoanalytic terminology into her teaching and criticism, and it was in her analysis of the work of Richardson in *The Egoist*, in 1918, that she introduced 'stream of consciousness' as a literary term. Prior to this, she was known for her reviews and criticism of the imagist poets, including H.D., Aldington and Pound, with whom she also socialized. Freud influenced the design and content of her fiction, and while May Sinclair published many works in her lifetime, most notable are two postwar novels: *The Life and Death of Harriett Frean* (1920) and *Mary Olivier: A Life* (1919). Indebted to the 'New Psychology', both novels are concerned with the life of women constrained by Victorian convention.

Mary Olivier identifies Christianity as one of the ideological ties that bind. For example, within the section on 'Adolescence', Mary discovers the idea of pantheism, that god is in everything, in the work of the seventeenth-century thinker Spinoza. Mary reflects: 'The God of Baruch Spinoza was the God you had wanted, the only sort of God you cared to think about. Thinking about him – after the Christian God – was like coming out of a small dark room into an immense open space filled with happy light' (Sinclair 1949: 100). In this passage, Sinclair uses a highly unusual second-person indirect narration to give the reader access to Mary's inner thoughts. The simile used at the end of this section emphasizes the contrast between Mary's perception of conventional Christianity and Spinoza's pantheism. The two images, which represent the religions, are starkly different: Christianity is the 'small dark room', while pantheism is 'an immense open space filled with happy light.' Mary's preference can be seen in the dichotomies between the 'dark/happy light' and the 'small room/ immense open space'. There is also the suggestion of a journey, symbolizing her new 'religious awakening' out of the confining room into the open air.

Tension also exists between Mary and her mother in relation to religion and education: Mary's mother is traditional in her outlook, while Mary seems to view herself in more progressive terms. This is implied in an exchange between the two women when Mary expresses a desire to read classical literature, which her mother calls 'silly vanity'. Sinclair describes how 'Mary's heart made a queer and startling movement, as if it turned over and dashed itself against her ribs. There was a sudden swelling and aching in her throat. Her head swam slightly. ... The person sitting on the yellow-painted bedroom chair was a stranger'. (Sinclair 1949: 126–7) Mary's reaction to her mother's opposition is a physical and, in a way, a violent one. Sinclair seems to be using images generally associated with heartbreak within a romantic relationship, which would be ironic considering the object of her desire is not focused upon a man, but an opportunity men have: a classical education, which at this time would have been the province of men. By contrast, her mother's traditional attitudes render her a stranger to Mary.

A kind of stream-of-consciousness effect, signalled by a change in narrative perspective at different times within the text, is used to give the reader an insight into the workings of Mary Olivier's mind and to indicate a shift from the 'objective' outer world to a 'subjective' inner one. For example, this is evident here in changes in register and narrative perspective:

You could see Uncle Victor's on the top, then Maurice Jourdain's. You heard the click of her tongue that dismissed those useless, unimportant things. The slim yellow letter at the bottom was Miss Lambert's. ...

... The poor, kind woman. The kind, dead woman. Years ago dead; her poor voice rising up, a ghostlike wail over your 'unbelief.' That was only the way she began. (Sinclair 1949: 323)

It is Mary's 'inner voice' and her sense of disbelief the reader hears in comments such as 'The poor, kind woman. The kind, dead woman.'

As in *Mary Olivier*, in *The Life and Death of Harriett Frean* the self-sacrificing behaviour of the protagonist encapsulates Sinclair's criticism of nineteenth-century value systems and their consequences. Harriett relinquishes Robin, her lover, to her best friend, and the renunciation leads them all towards frustrated lives. In a conversation with Robin, before his marriage to Prissie, they argue:

'You think of Prissie. You don't think of me.'
'Because it would *kill* her.'
'How about you?'
'It can't kill us, because we know we love each other. Nothing can take that from us.'
'But I couldn't be happy with her, Hatty. She wears me out. She's so restless.'
'*We* couldn't be happy, Robin. We should always be thinking of what we did to her.

How could we be happy?'
'You know how.'
'Well, even if we were, we've no right to get our happiness out of her suffering.'
'Oh, Hatty, why are you so good, so good?'
'I'm not good. It's only – there are some things you can't do. We couldn't. We couldn't.'

(Sinclair 1980: 61–2)

The result of this stance is Harriett's unhappiness and Prissie's depression in a loveless marriage to Robin. Sinclair implies that female self-sacrifice is counterproductive, in contrast to the calls for self-determination and enfranchisement advocated by the suffragette movement. Similarly, the story repeatedly implies Harriett's fear of sex and her indeterminate sexuality. Repressed sexuality and even sexual abuse are hinted at, making the novella an important contribution to feminist critiques of patriarchal Victorianism, alongside such earlier American works as Charlotte Perkins Gilman's *The Yellow Wallpaper* (1892) and Kate Chopin's *The Awakening* (1899).

CHAPTER THREE

1920s

INTRODUCTION

The 1920s are usually seen as the high point in Anglo-American modernism. The *annus mirabilis* of 1922 alone saw the publication of many remarkable works, including *The Waste Land, Ulysses, The Garden Party and Other Stories, The Life and Death of Harriett Frean, The Beautiful and the Damned, Jacob's Room,* Claude McKay's *Harlem Shadows,* T. E. Lawrence's extraordinary war memoir *Seven Pillars of Wisdom,* Eugene O'Neill's play *The Hairy Ape* and E. E. Cummings's autobiographical novel *The Enormous Room.* What all these works have in common is an attempt to make sense of the modern world through art, to fashion chaos into literature, and to provide an aesthetic coherence to formless reality. As E. M. Forster put it somewhat later: '[Art] is valuable because it has to do with order, and creates little worlds of its own, possessing internal harmony, in the bosom of this disordered planet. It is needed at once and now' (Forster 1965: 68).

Modernism moved away from representation in the Victorian sense of depicting the world, and towards a deep concern with the methods of representation. If art was a window on experience, the concern was now firmly on the role played by 'the window': language, form, narration, and perspective. Change and the perpetual movement of modern life seemed to emphasize impressions, transience, and shifting realities over the certainties of the previous century. As evident in D. H. Lawrence's 1921 work *Psychoanalysis and the Unconscious,* many of the artists and writers of the time were influenced by relativity and psychoanalysis, science and technology, the theories of thinkers and scientists such as Bergson, Planck, and Heisenberg.

What was to become the avant-garde in art had parallels with the avant-garde in engineering and architecture – interest in a faster movement through urban and rural landscapes, compressing space and creating a more intense experience of time. 'Cars, cars, fast, fast! One is seized, filled with enthusiasm, with joy ... the joy of power. The simple and naive pleasure of being in the midst of power, of strength' wrote the architect Le Corbusier in 1924. As Einstein revolutionized humanity's theoretical understanding of the universe, modern engineering revolutionized its experience of time and space. Reality was now relative to the individual's own velocity and position.

A concern with character and self accompanies this fascination with relativism, which often surfaced in scepticism and irony. The internal landscape of the mind and the self appeared to be largely uncharted territory in fiction. The old, stable ego now seemed fragmented and multifaceted. The new 'relative reality' perhaps existed in the mind and might be as myriad as the human beings who experienced it.

In terms of poetry, despite the emergence of imagism, verse was still predominantly Georgian after the war. The formally progressive war poets had not made their impact, Eliot was still hardly known, Ezra Pound was positioned with the avant-garde, and Yeats was not yet writing poetry that would be associated with modernism, despite his interest in symbolism. Eliot's popularization of a new kind of poetry with *The Waste Land*, edited by and dedicated to Ezra Pound, would, however, be decisive in moving away from prewar verse forms. Pound argued that the first task of the new poetry was to break the hold of the iambic pentameter; the fragmentation of metre that resulted, as witnessed by Eliot's poem, can be seen as a sign of the times – evidence of a world breaking free from the constraints of Edwardian society.

Delving into consciousness and exploring interiority became the hallmarks of modernist fiction, exemplified by Woolf and Joyce, but events of the decade were still reflected across literature. In Britain, the aftermath of the war was at the forefront of most minds, and few works of the decade ignored its impact any more than Irish writers like Yeats could fail to reflect on Independence and the Irish Civil War in the early 1920s. The vote for women (over the age of 21) in 1928 was followed by Woolf's important feminist lectures, published as *A Room of One's Own* in 1929, while *Ulysses* told a story of Irish history, Anglo-Irish relations, colonial migrancy and racial tensions, alongside its more esoteric concerns with Jesuitical philosophy.

In the United States, F. Scott Fitzgerald ushered the Jazz Age into literature with his first novels, *This Side of Paradise* (1920) and, especially, *The Beautiful and Damned* (1922). The American decade is famous for flappers and the Charleston, decadence and consumption, accompanied by prohibition and followed by the Wall Street crash in 1929, leading to the Great Depression of the 1930s. The Roaring Twenties was also notable for the Harlem Renaissance, an unprecedented flowering of black creativity across the arts and culture, as well as the growing artistic influence of the expatriate community in Europe, sketched in Ernest Hemingway's first novel, *The Sun Also Rises* (1926) and later in Fitzgerald's *Tender is the Night* (1934).

WOMEN IN LOVE (1920)

Women in Love marked a transitional moment in D. H. Lawrence's writing, as his novels turned more philosophical and darkly psychological. Nietzsche loomed still larger in his depiction of human will, evident in the intellectual, emotional, and physical lives of his characters. Though never addressed directly, the Great War sits at the heart of the novel's concern for a crisis in Western civilization and violence within human relationships.

Set again in and around the mining communities of the Midlands, the novel was conceived as the second half of *The Rainbow* in a long work to be entitled *The Sisters*. Length and obscenity laws led to *Women in Love* appearing several years after the earlier work, ostensibly as a separate novel. Continuing from *The Rainbow* the story of the latest generation of Brangwens, the novel follows the lives of Ursula and Gudrun Brangwen and their respective love affairs with Rupert Birkin and Gerald Crich. The four are interested in questions of how to live and the proper relationship between men and women, most thoroughly debated by the arguments of Birkin, who ties himself and others in knots of language as he tries to define 'equilibrium' between lovers.

The four represent deeply contrasting personalities: Ursula is a teacher at the mining town of Beldover, which was modelled on Lawrence's birthplace of Eastwood in Nottinghamshire; Gudrun is an artist back from her London school; Birkin is an independent-thinking school inspector partly based on Lawrence himself; and Gerald is an industrialist, the son of a local pit owner. In plot terms, the arc of the narrative includes the deaths of Gerald's sister and father, Ursula and Birkin's marriage, and finally Gerald's suicide in the alps after Gudrun begins a relationship with a German sculptor, Loerke. While others in the novel are too preoccupied with intellectual will, Gerald represents the physical mastery of nature, bending it to his purposes. His thrust towards mechanization and mineral exploitation has created the contemporary world, but this is shown to be out of step with the rhythms of nature and the wider needs of animals, including humans. Thus, modern love is depicted as a struggle for power between a man and a woman, or between two men in the novel's homoerotic wrestling scene, and is shown to be ultimately unsatisfying. Similarly, the novel begins with Ursula and Gudrun deciding marriage can never bring them happiness and ends with Ursula and Birkin disagreeing over whether monogamy can be fulfilling without accompanying strong same-sex relationships.

Recognizing that deeper psychological drives and needs beneath the conscious mind appear to offer a way through conventional society's ills, socially and personally, Lawrence provides no resolution in the novel, which ends in dispute, uncertainty, and Gerald's self-destruction as an emblem of the European death drive. Its modernist aspects stand out through its interest in linguistic exploration, interiority and psychological realism, depicting life revolving around characters and relationships more than plot and action. With *Women in Love* Lawrence breaks free from the prewar family novel and from Victorian convention in a way that several other novelists, particularly women, sought to in the period, but Lawrence also blends this with an innovative formal approach that emphasizes cycles of free thought and interrelation, rather than linear development and progress over time. As he writes in his critique of Western intellectualism and materialism, *Apocalypse*:

> To appreciate the pagan manner of thought we have to drop our manner of on-and-on-and-on, from a start to a finish, and allow the mind to move in cycles, or to flit here and there over a cluster of images. Our idea of time as a continuity in an eternal, straight line has crippled our consciousness cruelly. The pagan conception of time is much freer, it allows movement upwards and downwards, and allows for a complete change of the state of mind, at any moment. One cycle finished we can drop or rise to another level, and be in a new world at once. (Lawrence 1974: 54)

In addition to his literary works, Lawrence's contributions to the modernist novel were critical essays written in the 1920s, though some were not published until his nonfictional prose was collected under the title *Phoenix* in 1936, several years after his death. The most cited essays are 'The Novel' (1925), 'Morality and the Novel' (1925), 'Why the Novel Matters' (mid-1920s) and 'Surgery for the Novel – or a Bomb' (1923). In these essays, Lawrence, like Woolf, asserts his belief in 'life', though he defines it differently, as 'something that gleams, that has the fourth-dimensional quality' ('Morality and the Novel'). In 'Why the Novel Matters', he explains how he thinks the novelist deals with more of 'life' than the philosopher, the scientist, or even the poet:

> Nothing is important but life. ... For this reason I am a novelist. ... The novel is the one bright book of life. Books are not life. They are only tremulations on the ether. But the novel as a tremulation can make the whole man tremble. Which is more than poetry, philosophy, science, or any other book-tremulation can do. (Lawrence 1971: 184–5)

In his later work, Lawrence rediscovers the alternative cyclical movement of time outside Europe that, in works like *The Rainbow*, he had located in the English agricultural past. This is opposed to the industrial age, represented by Gerald in *Women in Love*: 'his body, his motion, his life – it was the same ticking, the same twitching ... across the eternal, mechanical monotonous clock-face of time' (Lawrence 1986: 564–5).

Where W. B. Yeats saw cyclical movements in Western history, marked by the fall of Troy, the rise of Christianity, and the epochal turmoil of the early twentieth century, Lawrence perceived an ethnic-racial revolution, as power would return to older civilizations that the West had dominated through superior technology. He writes in *Mornings in Mexico* that 'I don't believe in evolution, like a long string hooked on to a First Cause, and being slowly twisted in unbroken continuity through the ages. I prefer to believe in what the Aztecs called Suns: that is, Worlds successively created and destroyed.' (Lawrence 1960: 12). In this alternative tradition, while many other novelists looked to Bergson's psychological concept of duration, Lawrence appropriated colonial spaces to represent an escape from the tyranny of Western time.

THE GARDEN PARTY (1922)

Katherine Mansfield had been diagnosed with tuberculosis during the war, and she knew that she was dying at the time she composed the stories in *The Garden Party*. The most well-known piece in the collection is the title story, centred on a fatality that happens just as a party is to be thrown by the Sheridan family at their house. During preparations for the event, the Sheridans hear of the tragic death of a carter in the village; a horse had shied at a traction engine and the man had struck his head when thrown. This does not impact on the party directly, but one of the Sheridan daughters, Laura, goes to pay condolences to the bereaved Scott family. She is sent with leftovers from the party. The story concludes with Laura's confused thoughts on returning from the sight of the dead man's corpse in the bedroom of his house. All she has thought to say before the dead body is 'Forgive my hat', and the story ends in a failed epiphany as she attempts to put into words what she has felt. She tries to articulate her view of life, but falters as her stunted 'Isn't life –' echoes an earlier song featured in the story: 'This Life is Weary'.

For Mansfield, the story particularly pointed out the way in which life's events do not happen in any comprehensible order, which is disconcerting for a child. Laura is struck by the poor timing of the carter's death on the day of their carefully prepared garden party, and this violates her sense and desire for the comfort of order. On a day when Laura continues to be groomed in the ways of her mother and on how to treat others appropriately, the intrusion of bereavement, with the emotions it raises, jars with her feeling of social propriety and, perhaps, with her family's sense of hierarchy, sitting above the poor families in the lane: 'The very smoke coming out of their chimneys was poverty-stricken. Little rags and shreds of smoke, so unlike the great silvery plumes that uncurled from the Sheridans' chimneys' (Mansfield, 254). Here the story outlines a logic, which will be undercut, of binary difference between life and death, innocence and experience, upper and lower class. The attempted control of nature by staging a party in the garden is also indicative of life's unpredictabilities, especially as the weather and everything else augurs well for the event before the accident intrudes.

Drawing on a similar event in Mansfield's own childhood, 'The Garden Party' juxtaposes the rich and the poor in New Zealand, though the setting could as well be Europe. Unusually for such stories,

Mansfield shows the rich observing the poor, rather than the other way around. Like Mansfield, Laura thinks 'one must go everywhere, one must see everything', but the Sheridan women in the story appear to be groomed solely to be hostesses, party givers. This sense of donning a social role, together with the wider theme of identity, is represented by the new hat Laura contemplates before the mirror and apologizes for at the end. The element of self-regard is in contrast to the social role she might perform with respect to the poor families living close by, and the hat thus becomes an image of her sense of guilt as well as her social standing and her class's concern with appearance. She is class-bound (and consequently surprised that workmen might like the smell of lavender), but sufficiently self-conscious and reflective to see more than her own finery. She will have to accept that the gulf between classes cannot be easily bridged, but she is willing to contemplate the other sides to existence, unlike her mother, who does not want her party spoiled by talk of 'people of that class'.

The narration of the story operates through a mix of first and third person narration in a free indirect style of discourse: 'Again, how curious, she seemed to be different from them all. To take scraps from their party. Would the poor woman really like that?' (Mansfield: 258) In this way, the reader accesses Laura's thoughts, but in the third person, leaving it ambiguous as to whether these are the words in Laura's mind or an approximation of her thoughts. The principal device the story uses is one of ellipsis, where thoughts and speech trail off, allowing the reader to complete or leave unfinished the character's expression. Such a refusal to direct the reader is reflected also in the way the stories often begin in the middle of something, as here: 'And after all the weather was ideal'. It also indicates the lack of a vocabulary to express unconventional thoughts in this society, as well as the social taboos on language. The latter is evident in Mrs Sheridan's view that it was 'tactless' of her husband to mention the dead man's large and nearby family, while she herself bites her tongue when talking to Laura because it is better not to 'put such ideas in the child's head!'.

Other important stories in the collection are 'At the Bay', a sequel to 'Prelude' from *Bliss and Other Stories*, 'Miss Brill', 'The Stranger' and 'The Daughters of the Late Colonel'. This last story is superficially an upper-class comedy of domestic manners, satirizing an aesthetic of leisure-class boredom. Underneath, like *The Good Soldier*, it can be seen as an articulation of the crises exposed by the

Great War, bringing to the surface Victorian social and cultural mores in a colonial context. While expressing no clear feminist views, the story – through its rhetorical questions, ellipses and pro-crastinations – shows the repression, fear and desolation of two sisters both freed and yet imprisoned by the death of their father.

Mansfield died in March 1923. Indicating both her talent and potential, Virginia Woolf wrote: 'I was jealous of her writing... the only writing I have ever been jealous of.'

ULYSSES (1922)

Everything in Joyce's novel has been seen to be multireferential. The book is a social, linguistic, cultural and political matrix of wordplay, allusions, cross-references and multilayered palimpsests, from its early pages set in one of Dublin's fortified Martello Towers to its conclusion in the Blooms' bedroom with Molly's soliloquy, frequently taken to be the foremost example of stream of consciousness writing.

On the one hand, *Ulysses* has been most easily approached through its Homeric parallels with the *Odyssey*, on to whose sections the 18 chapters loosely map, or through its precise episodic encoding of time, place, symbol, colour, body part, and literary technique. There are other linguistic, literary and formal approaches to the book that dominated most early critical reception of it as the exemplary modernist novel, which needed to be read with the kind of attention more normally reserved for the density of poetry.

On the other hand, recent social and political readings have come to the fore and suggested the richness of less formalistic approaches to the text. To start with, it is hard to ignore the significance of the fact that Joyce's novel was published in the year Ireland was partitioned: 1922. Rooted in Dublin, which Joyce described as the second city of the British Empire, *Ulysses*'s concern with 'racial' identity and xenophobia, nationalism and anti-colonialism has long been commented upon within critical studies, yet studies with a strong focus on race, empire and nation(alism) have appeared only since the 1990s. Underlining the polyphonic quality of Joyce's writing, *Ulysses* as a text has responded strongly to all schools of critical thinking since the 1960s, and, for example, the influence of Edward Said's *Orientalism* and of postcolonial studies is now found across the range of work on Joyce, which is now almost as likely to reference the novel's representation of black or Jewish identity as contemporary Irish concerns at the time of the novel's composition, such as the Celtic Revival, the Land League and the Easter Rising. The book's engagement with English occupation in its early chapters, its various perspectives on nationalism and ethnic identity in the middle chapters, and its constant toying with racial representations and colonial allusions, make *Ulysses* as rich a text for postcolonial analyses as it has proved for other critical approaches. Ultimately, *Ulysses* is a polyphonic, multicultural text without final authority, anchored by no fixed convictions of generic, narratorial or authorial integrity.

The book also sits in a network with Joyce's other fictional texts. For example, characters from *Dubliners* reappear: Bob Doran, the boarding house tenant entrapped into marrying the landlady's daughter, is now a henpecked drunk, offering a conclusion to the earlier story, but he is also presented as less than the sympathetic character he seemed in the earlier collection, rewriting our first impression of him. Of the three central characters in *Ulysses*, two are new, Leopold and Molly Bloom, but the third is Stephen Dedalus, the protagonist of *A Portrait of the Artist as a Young Man*. Having fled Ireland at the end of the earlier novel, Stephen is now back in Dublin in June 1904 following his mother's death. As Stephen and Bloom traipse the city, Joyce faithfully details its public minutiae, textually rebuilding Dublin with painstaking accuracy. In contrast to the coherence suggested by this painstaking recreation of the great European modernist city in the depiction of Dublin, many early influential critics of the novel, such as F. R. Leavis, found that in its linguistic and aesthetic diversity, as well as its peripatetic plotting, *Ulysses* lacked coherence and unity. To an extent, this resulted in Joyce being more commonly situated in the European literary canon than in Leavis's 'English great tradition'.

Ulysses takes place on one day, and its 18 chapters roughly map onto hours, starting at eight in the morning. In *Ulysses*, Joyce intended to create an 'everyman' figure in Bloom, his Irish-Jewish Odysseus, who is presented in minute detail in the majority of the novel's chapters. The first three chapters, however, are devoted to Stephen Dedalus, Joyce's fictional alter ego. Returned from Paris after his mother's death, Stephen is now a thoughtful, somewhat morose young man teaching at a school in Dalkey. The novel's Homeric parallel is predicated on Stephen as Telemachus, loyal son awaiting Ulysses's return. The father figure Stephen will find is Bloom. In the fourth chapter, Bloom rises and prepares breakfast for his wife, who remains in bed. He thinks of their daughter Milly in Mullingar, then visits the post office, where he receives a romantic letter from a woman with whom he has been flirtatiously corresponding. He then attends Paddy Dignam's funeral, visits a newspaper office (he is an advertising salesman), has dinner in a hotel, drops into a pub, and so on. Later in the day, he meets with Stephen, they visit a brothel and Stephen accompanies Bloom home for cocoa before departing.

The final chapter is devoted to the rendition of Molly Bloom's internal thoughts. She is, in the end, a faithful Penelope in her heart. After a sexual liaison earlier in the day she now meditates on her life growing up as Marion Tweedy and her decision to marry Leopold Bloom, which decision is joyously endorsed in the novels closing words of affirmation.

In an early review, T. S. Eliot concluded that Joyce's technique in Ulysses had made the modern world possible for art. Utilizing the scale of myth and classical allusion gave strength to a lightweight modern world. Form, order, and symbol, stalwarts of modernist technique, were the controlling mechanisms to shape the chaos of modern experience epitomized by the waste and terror of the recently ended war, providing 'a significance to the immense panorama of futility and anarchy which is contemporary history' (Eliot 1923).

THE WASTE LAND (1922)

In *The Waste Land*, as in his reading of Joyce's *Ulysses*, Eliot turned to a controlling 'mythical method' to bring artistic order to the perceived turmoil of modern life. In a famous essay on 'The Metaphysical Poets' (1921) he had already advanced these ideas in relation to the history of poetry and identified what he termed a 'dissociation of sensibility' in the seventeenth century. In the work of Donne and Shakespeare, Eliot found a unity of thought and feeling that he believed was subsequently missing in poetry, which became increasingly vague and emotional by the nineteenth century. With his 'objective correlative', glossed in the later chapter, and impersonal 'mythical method', Eliot thus sought to turn from the models of Romanticism to those of classicism and to reintroduce a combination of intelligence and wit to poetry, uniting feeling and thought once more.

The fragments of the poem are held together by its narrator, who orchestrates the different voices and assembles the pieces into a whole.

Eliot sees the poet, in typically modernist fashion, as an orderer of disarray, but there is a kind of relativity here that insists on the import-ance of the observer who sees, for example, 'fear in a handful of dust'. This approach is most evident in formation of the entire poem, in which nothing is literal, but everything is described in terms of its meaning to the assembler of the fragments, who Eliot says is the blind seer Tiresias, who knows all the past and apprehends all the future. Through Tiresias, who has been both man and woman, modern sex is viewed in terms of Elizabethan courtship, and the crowds of business people marching over London Bridge are related to the trade routes of the ancient Mediterranean. Meaning is shifted into the eye of the beholder, and the reader cannot locate a meaning but, similarly, has to construct one. Again Eliot's theory of the 'objective correlative', taken from the nineteenth-century artist Washington Allston, comes in here. He wrote in his 1919 essay 'Hamlet and His Problems' that 'The only way of expressing emotion in the form of art is by finding an 'object-ive correlative'; in other words, a set of objects, a situation, a chain of events which shall be the formula of that particular emotion.' Lan-guage is to be used to describe an 'internal reality' which for many modernists replaces the external social reality foregrounded by nine-teenth-century literature. Poetry "expresses emotion' through objects, situations, and events, and the presentation here in *The Waste Land* is from someone who is split between conscious and unconscious; who constructs a personal, internal meaning; who is inadequately repre-sented in language; and who is alienated in the modern city.

Eliot's poem is often taken to be exemplary of modernist poetics, for a number of reasons. First, because it treats the present through mythology (from vegetation rites to Egyptian mythology to Wagner's Gods). As Joyce's *Ulysses* uses Greek mythology to impose a struc-ture on modern formless life, so Eliot employs such myths as that of the Fisher King from Frazer's *The Golden Bough*. Eliot uses the con-trast between modern life and the ancient, the Greek, and even the Elizabethan world order as a way to criticize meaningless disorder in the contemporary world. He, of course, does this through the fragmentation of the poem, but its use of myth and allegory is also indicative.

The poem is additionally characteristic of modernism in its inter-est in time, which is apparently unrelated to history. So, in *The Waste Land*, Eliot deals with a destroyed postwar Europe, but there is not a single direct reference to the war or to any fact of social change.

Modernist writers frequently declared themselves to be unconcerned with history, but this means that history and politics are repressed within their writing, which is in itself a significant historical effect.

The typically modernist sense of fragmentation is apparent in *The Waste Land*'s broken images, scraps of language, and allusions to ruins, but also in the way the poem plays out a number of scenes on just a few themes of sex and death. Plus, it is a poem of urban scenes, illustrating why modernism is often considered the literature of city life. Novelists of the nineteenth century, such as Dickens, George Eliot, and Gaskell, treat urban culture as a contrast to life in the country – the city as a place of poverty and industrialization – but the modernists deal with technological change, with offices and traffic, advertising and shopping, and the entire metropolitan ideal of a fast and compact social and cultural life that is not contrasted with a provincial life, but supersedes it with its crowds, mass entertainment, apartment blocks, and miles of concrete. For the modernist writer, this is the collective contemporary reality that has to be expressed amid the ruins of Europe, along with the new experiences of anonymity, of being lonely in a crowd, of being surrounded and alienated.

As well as postwar ruins and fragmented characters held together in symbols, there are also linguistic fragments: quotations, snatches of song, phrases from different languages, numerous myths. There is again here a tension between unity and disunity: the narrative ends with fragments and ruins, but of course the poem itself strives to remain whole. The form of the verse aims to piece together or reconcile the jigsaw of the allusions, half-lines, non sequiturs and quotations of the language. All sorts of peripheral machinery around the poem are put in place, seemingly to try to hold in the chaos: the endnotes, the Greek epigraph, the five sections like acts in a tragedy.

Typical of the postwar period, Eliot has expressions of apocalypse and crisis that represent modernism's own condition as a radical break, but there is also an attempt to rebuild the 'ruins' through aesthetic form. The poem, or to Eliot the mind of the poet, is the site on which this knitting together, this reconstruction can take place. E. M. Forster maintained that the purpose of art was to make order out of chaos, and as we saw, he used the motto 'only connect' for *Howards End* in 1910 because he felt the modern world was dividing between haves and have-nots, between culture and materialism, men and women, city and country. In his notes, Eliot says the poem is partly about the crisis in Europe. In the years following the First World War, Western civilization seemed to have failed, to need rethinking, as in *Women in Love*, as well as rebuilding. The rebirth at the start of the poem appears to suggest this: after the winter of war, the pain of rehabilitation and spring regrowth must take place. This is also the message of the central binding myth from Frazer behind the poem: of the wounded fisher king whose impotence is matched by that of the land.

Eliot wrote in 'The Metaphysical Poets' in 1921:

> A poet's mind ... is constantly amalgamating experience; the ordinary man's experience is chaotic, irregular, fragmentary. The latter falls in love, or reads Spinoza, and these two experiences have nothing to do with each other, or with the smell of cooking; in the mind of the poet these experiences are always forming new wholes. (Eliot 1974: 117)

What the poem also aims to convey is that order is not on the surface. This is another preoccupation of the modernists who sought deep structures – myth, the unconscious – to contain meaning. The poem has no coherence in its literal meanings, but it has one through the connectedness of literature, culture and myth.

As first discussed in relation to Conrad, another important failure for the modernists involves language. On the one hand, modernists no longer felt they could express reality transparently through language, as the Victorians had. On the other hand, modernists generally did not doubt that there was a reality of some kind to be expressed, as postmodernist theory does. The failure sat with the means of expression, with words which, Eliot says, slip and slide, which are only fragments of a reality that exists inside the mind.

A PASSAGE TO INDIA (1924)

Published 14 years after his previous novel, *A Passage to India* was the last full-length fictional work E. M. Forster felt he could write. Between his first visit to India in 1912 and his second in 1921, Forster's novel gestated in his mind over a ten-year period. In terms of style, it differs considerably from his earlier work, introducing symbols and a metaphysical dimension as well as the overt political setting in British-ruled India.

Though it takes place before the narrative begins, the principal physical 'passage' in the novel is that of Adela Quested and Mrs Moore, who have travelled by sea from England to visit Ronny Heaslop, the

City magistrate at Chandrapore, a seemingly unremarkable Indian town. Heaslop is engaged to Adela and is the son of Mrs Moore's first marriage. Mrs Moore is a spiritual figure with a similar significance to Ruth Wilcox in Forster's previous novel, *Howards End*. Adela is a serious-minded, callow young woman keen to see, in the earnest but naïve manner of a tourist, the 'real India'.

The first key meeting or symbolic passage to India of the novel is Mrs Moore's encounter at a Mosque by the Ganges with the Muslim doctor Aziz, the book's Indian protagonist. The next attempt at connection, at Indo-British friendship, is the failed 'Bridge Party', which the city's standoffish officials arrange so that the two visiting women can meet the local Indian community. By contrast, the third meeting of the novel's first part, 'Mosque', is an unofficial get-together organized by Cyril Fielding, a liberal college principal, at whose home congregate Adela, Mrs Moore, Aziz and the Hindu Brahmin Professor Godbole. However, this party at Fielding's is also soured when Ronny arrives and ruins the atmosphere with his high-handed sahib demeanour. Set during India's cold season, the section overall has been characterized by attempts at, mostly, good-natured hospitality and invitation undermined by Anglo-Indian prejudice as well as cultural difference and misunderstanding which Forster presents in terms of the English dislike of 'muddle'.

The middle section of the novel is set up by Aziz inviting the group gathered at Fielding's to be his guests on a later occasion. 'Caves' is set in the hot weather, and its principal subject is the journey to the famous and extraordinary Marabar Caves, which Aziz is obliged to undertake, despite everyone's lethargy over the prospect. The trip is dogged by false starts and unpleasantness, as Fielding misses the train and Mrs Moore feels physically and spiritually unwell in the first cave they visit. Adela and Aziz continue alone with only a guide to a second group of caves and become separated after a moment of embarrassment caused by Adela asking Aziz if he has more than one wife. They enter separate caves, but shortly afterwards Adela rushes down the hill to stop a car and return to Chandrapore. Though the reader will never know what actually happened, Adela believes she has been assaulted in the caves by Dr Aziz.

Fielding and Mrs Moore believe Aziz to be innocent, but the rest of the Anglo-Indian community rallies behind Adela and Ronny. Fielding is ostracized by the other members of the raj and resigns from the English club. Mrs Moore decides to sail home, and she dies aboard ship, news of the event reaching the others shortly after Aziz's trial. In the courtroom, Adela realizes and admits that she has made a mistake; Aziz is acquitted. She is shunned by the English, but Fielding decides to support her, though his friendship with Aziz suffers as a result. Aziz thinks that a romance is developing between Adela and Fielding, but the two sail home to England separately.

Two years later, the scene shifts to Mau, where Godbole is Minister of Education and Aziz is doctor to the Rajah. It is now the rainy season, and the final section, 'Temple', starts with a description of the Gokul Ashtami festival, celebrating the birth of Krishna, at which Godbole officiates. Fielding arrives back in India and is on tour with his wife and her brother. He has come to Mau to inspect the local school. Aziz has no desire to meet him, as he believes Fielding to have wed Adela, though he has actually married Mrs Moore's daughter from her second marriage, Stella. Aziz is only calmed when he meets Stella's diffident brother Ralph, who has the same spiritual qualities, as well as openness and goodwill, that Aziz responded to in Mrs Moore. Aziz's reconciliation with Fielding is achieved when their boats collide on the Mau Tank at the height of the festival and each falls into the water. The famous ending of the novel has them riding together in the jungle, still wishing to be friends, but aware that the political situation makes it impossible in the here and now.

Two elements to the book illustrate its modernist features: rhythm and symbolism. The quasi-musical use of rhythm, repeated phrases, cadences and images is discussed later in this study in relation to Forster's *Aspects of the Novel*; however, all of the book is highly structured to create patterns and repetitions. To begin with, it has a three-part structure in the sections 'Mosque', 'Caves', 'Temple', which are Indian spaces respectively representing Islam, Jainism (a fifth-century BC atheistic religion) and Hinduism. The book also follows a seasonal pattern in its three parts, from cold weather to hot weather to the rains.

Another key element to the book's construction is the central symbol of the caves, which has been interpreted in many ways. First, they appear hollow, empty spaces to match Forster's perception of metaphysical emptiness in a Godless universe. Second, they arguably match an Orientalist view of India as a place of mystery and nullity. Third, the hollow caves can be read as a symbol of the main textual absence in the book, its missing centre: the enigma of what happened to Adela.

If we move to a wider consideration of the book, in one respect, the narrative concerns Adela's quest to discover 'the real India.' What she actually finds is the Marabar hills, and an accompanying atmosphere of sexual fear and human inconsequence in the universe. There are arguments which say that India is reduced to the Marabar Caves in the novel. Everything we learn about the caves applies also to European views of the country: they are dark, empty, oppressive, and mysterious. The common Western habit of imagining India as a land occupied by monsoons, heat and dust, rather than people, is repeated in the fetishizing in the novel of the caves, which are presented as inexplicable and unknowable, remote and timeless.

Overall, the novel suggests Forster's view that politics is opposed to, or at least always in tension with, personal friendship. Forster aimed to make this a book about progressive, liberal-minded British and Indian people trying to be amicable against an antithetical backdrop of imperial rule and administration. The novel is therefore partly about what Forster and others have called the liberal dilemma: the opposition to political extremism and intolerance combined with a refusal to use force. Throughout the novel, the constant emphasis on 'goodwill', 'friendship' and 'tolerance' is an assertion of Forster's liberal creed, the erosion of which in the interwar years of rising totalitarianism may have contributed to Forster's decision to write no more novels.

MRS DALLOWAY (1925)

Virginia Woolf's fiction developed in complexity and depth over the 1920s. Her two pre-1920s novels, *The Voyage Out* and *Night and Day*, were comparatively conventional works when set beside her later ones. Only with *Jacob's Room* (1922) does a complex style emerge, one that immerses the reader in a fictional world that requires navigation. The opening page of *Mrs Dalloway* stresses this 'plunge': 'What a lark! What a plunge! For so it had always seemed to her, when, with a little squeak of the hinges, which she could hear now, she had burst open the French windows and plunged at Bourton into the open air.' (Woolf 1976: 5) This early paragraph illustrates not just how the reader is plunged into the story, but also how memory works for Woolf. The squeak of hinges plunges Mrs Dalloway back to her youth at Bourton and the character's thoughts inhabit the narrative as they do her own consciousness. The novel will also end with contemplation of a plunge, as a dive onto railings marks the death of the other principal character in the novel, ex-soldier Septimus Smith, who is obsessed with the past, just as Mrs Dalloway is.

Contemplation of Septimus's death will be a major instance of self-immersion for Clarissa Dalloway in the novel. Where Joyce makes use of the 'epiphany', an intense experience or even an insight into the self, Woolf employs what she calls 'the moment', a word that occurs repeatedly in *Mrs Dalloway*. Woolf depicts more of a physical feeling than Joyce does in his instant of spiritual insight, and, for example, there is this moment in Woolf's novel when Mrs Dalloway thinks she sometimes feels for women as men are meant to: 'for that moment, she had seen an illumination; a match burning in a crocus; an inner meaning almost expressed. But the close withdrew; the hard softened. It was over – the moment' (Woolf 1976: 30). This emotional instant is rendered in such vivid detail that its suggestive sensual imagery, like the flame inside a flower, can serve as a forging energy. 'The moment' is thus a method of connecting people through common intense emotion, and this is something Woolf's portrayal of thought also aims to include.

Joyce and Woolf are often similarly compared with regard to their use of 'stream of consciousness', though there are differences. As previously mentioned, the term itself originates with William James, brother of Henry, whose observation was that the mind proceeds like a river or stream, rather than in blocks like speech. Thought is fluid, flowing, associative, rather than structured, and not grammatical.

Woolf, in fact, uses a technique that is better described as interior monologue, in which the flow of thoughts is accompanied by qualifiers such as 'she thought' or 'he wondered'. Also, sentences, syntax, and vocabulary do not alter between characters as much as they do in Joyce's work, and this helps to connect characters. Woolf additionally uses the past tense for these soliloquies, to stress the importance of personal history, and metaphors for the process of thought are as common as the thoughts themselves. The effect of this is important in *Mrs Dalloway* because it allows the narrative to skip from character to character without appearing to make abrupt shifts. Woolf thus conveys what she calls 'life', which is to say the narrative can slide between different consciousnesses for purposes of comparison and connection.

Her technique is made more complex by Woolf's use of time. Throughout the novel, she contrasts public with private time, the social time of the clock with that of the individual consciousness. So, she may start to report a character's thoughts when a clock begins striking the hour, detail them for several pages and then return to an awareness of the clock finishing striking the hour. Like that of Stein, Sinclair and others, Woolf's technique is indebted to the insights of Henri Bergson, among other psychologists and philosophers, who distinguished between temporal duration in the mind and chronology.

In *Mrs Dalloway*, time is superficially structured around divisions of the clock. The novel was originally to be called 'The Hours' and the sounding of Big Ben, which breaks up the novel into hours and sections, provides the book with its only divisions. In this way, the internal mental time of the characters, the duration that is timed according to the memories and preconscious thoughts that are recalled to a surface reality, is interrupted by a shared time that connects the characters as the clock chimes in the air form links across London.

As suggested above, the major connection in *Mrs Dalloway* is that made, unknowingly to them, between Clarissa Dalloway and Septimus Smith. In her original conception of the novel, Woolf was to have Clarissa kill herself, but in the finished text it is the shell-shocked Septimus who plunges to his death on railings. Both characters have led lives oppressed by patriarchy and are forced to live their fullest existence internally. The difference between them is that Clarissa, 52-year-old wife of a Conservative Member of Parliament, can bring together the fragments of consciousness into a whole, whereas Septimus cannot focus on the present because he is unable to forget the death of his comrade Evans in the trenches.

Clarissa considers the sides of her personality as akin to sides of a multifaceted jewel that she can bring together to face the world. However, Septimus cannot perform this drawing together, and so lacks the ability to mould his fragments of self into a whole for the purposes of social interaction. The emphasis on social pressures is underlined by the novel's conclusion at Mrs Dalloway's party. This gathering together is Woolf's metaphor for everyday life, and it is what petrifies Septimus Smith: 'this drawing together of everything to one centre before his eyes, as if some horror had come almost to the surface and was about to burst into flames, terrified him' (Woolf 1976: 15).

Mrs Dalloway also presents a multiplanar view of reality in order to represent the complexity of the modern world. Woolf called her technique of constructing character 'tunnelling', by which she meant she would burrow into a character's past in order to unearth a history. Her characters are then revealed to the reader as beings living simultaneously in the past and the present. Their current thoughts tell us who they are, but only the presence of the past shaped in those thoughts explains them.

TO THE LIGHTHOUSE (1927)

Woolf's next novel was conceived as a tripartite structure with two blocks of space joined by a corridor of time: 'The Window', 'Time Passes', and 'The Lighthouse'. The book's single location is a house on the island of Skye, where a family sits out the summer away from London and welcomes assorted guests.

To an extent, the story is an elegy for Woolf's parents and for her own distant childhood, when she and her family would spend their summers at a house in St Ives on the Cornish coast. This was the time of greatest happiness in Woolf's life, but the holidays ceased after the death of her mother, Julia, when she was 13 years old.

To the Lighthouse is also a novel of transition that marks the passing from one world, and the art that represented it, to a postwar world with a new class structure and different aesthetics. The structural architecture of the book is imaged in Lily Briscoe's painting, a gradual assemblage of strokes that accumulate to show a whole artwork. That accumulation was to be through character portrayals, not plot or worldview, but the problems of artistic design are peppered throughout the novel, from Mr Ramsay's philosophical A to Z, to Lily's own difficulties: 'she could not achieve that razor-edge of balance between two opposite figures' (Woolf 2000: 209). *To the Lighthouse* is patterned and full of shapes, one of the most arranged of all the artfully constructed novels of the 1920s. It is also a book of subtexts, ellipses, parenthetical thoughts, and of ways of seeing, concerned with viewpoints: literal, emotional, and figurative. The book has a good deal to say through the mouths of its many passing figures, but character and atmosphere, rhythm and emotion, are the central aspects of the book, not action or opinion.

The subject of Lily's picture suggests to the reader Woolf's intention in shaping a novel from the memories she had of her own family when a child:

But the picture was not of them, she said. Or, not in his sense.
There were other senses too, in which one might reverence them.
By a shadow here and light there, for instance. Her tribute took
that form, if, as she vaguely supposed, a picture must be a tribute.
(Woolf 2000: 59)

The title of Part One, 'The Window', suggests its place and function as a lens through which the reader sees the Ramsay family and
their guests. It also expresses a sense of the Ramsays, especially the
children, looking out at the world, and particularly towards the lighthouse. It creates a frame through which is seen a prewar world.

Spanning the war, 'Time Passes' consists of ten dark, lyrical sections ticking through the ten years, roughly 1909 to 1918, that separate Parts One and Three. It is also the period that the house at the
heart of the book lies empty of people. The section draws a horizon-
tal thread across the book equivalent to the vertical line down the
centre of Lily's painting. For a novelist concerned primarily with
character, this was a difficult section for Woolf to write, devoid of
people, in an attempt at a new fictional form.

'The Lighthouse' is the culmination of the book. It recounts a
postwar gathering once more at the house, with Mrs Ramsay dead
and most of the children grown. Lily recalls her unfinished painting
and her problem about its foreground, then determines to finish it
now (Woolf 2000: 161). As journey's end and as symbol, 'The Lighthouse' is elusive and aspirational, suggestive but not simple. Instead
of allowing light simply to pass through, like a window of memory
onto childhood, it projects out a rhythmical pulsating light. The
lighthouse is a destination in life for the characters, an endpoint
finally reached as Lily finishes her painting and Woolf her 'vision' at
the novel's close:

With a sudden intensity, as if she saw it clear for a second, she
drew a line there, in the centre. It was done; it was finished. Yes,
she thought, laying down her brush in extreme fatigue, I have had
my vision. (Woolf 2000: 226)

ORLANDO (1928)

Written in homage to the life, ancestry, and home of her friend Vita
Sackville-West, Woolf's *Orlando* is a transgressive book of changes,

mutabilities and transcendence. The story begins in the age of Elizabeth I and closes in Woolf's present of the 1920s. Over the course of the centuries, her protagonist Orlando loves both men and women, cross-dresses, and changes sex, too. He begins as a man, changes sex in the latter part of the seventeenth century, and continues as a woman.

A fantastical fictional biography of a hermaphrodite, the book's tone is ironic. For example, Woolf's description of Orlando near the beginning of the text serves two purposes: first, she demonstrates her playful attitude towards her 'subject', and second, she seems to be subverting the biographical genre. Using the diction of the Elizabethan era, she comments on her hero:

> But, alas, that these catalogues of youthful beauty cannot end without mentioning forehead and eyes. Alas, that people are seldom born devoid of all three; for directly we glance at Orlando standing by the window, we must admit that he had eyes like drenched violets, so large that the water seemed to have brimmed in them and widened them ... (Woolf 2003: 6)

The repetition of 'alas,' once after 'But' and then at the beginning of the following sentence, has a bathetic effect, because in the preceding sentences Orlando has been fashioned as the epitome of 'youthful beauty'. The use of 'drenched violets' to describe his eyes is perhaps unflattering, yet witty, and hints at 'femininity': it is one of the first signs of Orlando's androgyny. The following comment also reminds the reader of the 'bad' biography introduced by fellow Bloomsbury-ite Lytton Strachey's debunking of *Eminent Victorians* in 1918: 'Directly we glance at eyes and forehead, we have to admit a thousand disagreeables which it is the aim of every good biographer to ignore' (Woolf 2003: 6). There is a critical subtext here, in that Woolf is implying biographers deliberately 'aim' to gloss over the truth by choosing to 'ignore' a person's less worthy or beautiful characteristics. The use of 'good' to describe such biographers seems to be ironic and at odds with Woolf's own viewpoint.

Unsurprisingly, gender is a major theme of this novel in which the main character actually changes from a man to a woman halfway through the text. When this transformation occurs, Woolf, as biographer, interrupts the narrative with the following observation:

> Orlando had become a woman there is no denying it. But in every other respect, Orlando remained precisely as he had been. The

change of sex, though it altered their future, did nothing whatever to alter their identity. (Woolf 2003: 67)

Orlando's 'sex' may have changed, but 'their identity' has not; Woolf implies men and women are innately individuals first and foremost, regardless of sex. The inclusion of the comment 'though it altered their future' within commas, serves as an afterthought of Woolf's, but highlights the different outcome of Orlando's life occasioned by the change in gender. The emphasis is particularly on the point that identity remains the same, despite the fact that he is now a she, and it is only society that will perceive an important difference.

These ideas are developed later in the text when Orlando converses with Shelmerdine, her male lover:

> For each was surprised at the quickness of the other's sympathy, and it was to each such a revelation that a woman could be as tolerant and free-spoken as a man, and a man as strange and subtle as a woman, that they had to put the matter to the proof at once. (Woolf 2003: 127)

It is perhaps also ironic that this new knowledge they gain from each other is to them a 'revelation.' Woolf seems to be destabilizing, or subverting, traditional notions of 'masculinity' and 'femininity,' saying that women have the potential to be 'masculine' and vice versa. The implication is that gender is a 'performance', underlined by Orlando's gender transformation taking place during a masque. Women may 'act out' society's conventional expectations of them, while possessing characteristics traditionally attributed to men – gender is acquired, or learned, rather than existing *ab initio*.

In another striking aspect of the novel, Woolf's presentation of time and modernity seems to draw on both futurism and Einstein's theory of relativity, as in the following extract towards the end of the novel:

> She ran downstairs, she jumped into her motor-car, she pressed the self-starter and was off. Vast blue blocks of building rose into the air; the red cowls of chimneys were spotted irregularly across the sky; the road shone like silver-headed nails; omnibuses bore down upon her with sculptured white-faced drivers; she noticed sponges, bird-cages, boxes of green American cloth. (Woolf 2003: 147–8)

The diction and punctuation of the first sentence is suggestive of Orlando running like an automatic machine, the pace of the phrasing quickening as though imitating the starting up of a car, while the use of verbs such as 'ran,' 'jumped' and 'pressed' imply action without thought. The next sentence almost entirely eschews a subject position and implies Orlando has fused with the car as one machine, speeding through a glimpsed cubist landscape. Again, Woolf's interest in the performance of identity, here in a context of mechanistic and relative motion, is brought to the fore, playfully underlining her concern with the plasticity of gender and sexuality in her previous novels of the 1920s.

A ROOM OF ONE'S OWN (1929)

Woolf's *A Room of One's Own* is a key feminist text that explores the relationship between women and literature and economics. It is a signal essay when considering the history of modernist studies after the Second World War, when very few female authors were admitted to the academy's discussion of modernism, and Woolf's reputation itself was quite low among critics. Not until the rise of second wave feminism from the late 1960s onwards did women modernists start to be published again, to be reappraised, and to be brought back into the canon of widely studied authors.

Three of Woolf's concerns illustrate the book's importance. The first is the idea of a 'room' itself and Woolf's 'opinion upon one minor point' when asked to speak at Cambridge in 1928 about 'Women and Fiction': 'a woman must have money and a room of her own if she is to write fiction.' (Woolf 1973: 6) The 'room' here is associated with economic independence, not just a space in which to write.

A second concern is revealed in Woolf's subsequent discussion of Judith Shakespeare. This is an imagined account of the life of a conjectured equally brilliant sister to the playwright and follows on from Woolf's observation that for social and economic reasons 'it would have been impossible, completely and entirely, for any woman to have written the plays of Shakespeare in the age of Shakespeare' (Woolf 1973: 46).

A third concern is with 'androgyny', which is important in several of Woolf's novels, but she most fully discusses the concept here in *A Room Of One's Own*. Woolf takes the term from the writings of

Coleridge, but develops it into a view that 'it is fatal for anyone who writes to think of their sex. It is fatal to be a man or woman pure and simple; one must be woman-manly or man-womanly' (Woolf 1973: 99). Woolf wonders 'whether there are two sexes in the mind corresponding to the two sexes in the body, and whether they also require to be united in order to get complete satisfaction and happiness ... in each of us two powers reside, one male , one female; and in the man's brain the man predominates over the woman, and in the woman's brain the woman predominates over the man.' (Woolf 1973: 93). Woolf's strategy appears to be to fuse all constructions of masculinity and femininity, of male or female behaviour, and to argue for a hybrid identity like Orlando's.

In *Mrs Dalloway*, to take another example, on the one hand there is the description of Peter Walsh as being a womanly man, and, on the other hand we are told of Clarissa's pleasure, which is like a man's, when kissing Sally Seton. In Clarissa's love for Sally and Septimus's hero-worship of Evans, we are arguably seeing different aspects of androgynous personalities: rather than reject the labels themselves, Woolf asserts that Clarissa has a masculine side and Septimus has a feminine one. This becomes more important when discussing the positioning of Septimus as a soldier lacking 'manly' courage – because of his reaction to shell-shock – by the Harley street doctors in the novel, Holmes and Bradshaw. So Woolf gives us the archetype of social masculinity, a soldier, and concentrates on the side of him that Western culture perceives as both aberrant and feminine: consequently, in the novel, Septimus himself also believes that men and their institutions could become more holistic and nurturing. Also, by linking Clarissa and Septimus emotionally and symbolically, but never physically, Woolf shows two sides to a single identity, and presents to us an androgynous composite figure. In this respect, *Mrs Dalloway* anticipates *Orlando*, yet *Mrs Dalloway* is a less radical text than *Orlando* and its strategy is to redefine feminine and masculine as aspects shared by men and women, rather than to attempt to reverse or expunge the categories altogether. Thinking about this in terms of modernist experimentation, the sexual division in the mind that Woolf terms 'androgyny' is seemingly just one part of her wider assault on the coherence and stability of unitary consciousness. She writes in *A Room of One's Own*:

What does one mean by 'the unity of the mind'? I pondered, for clearly the mind has so great a power of concentrating at any point at any moment that it seems to have no single state of being. It can separate itself from the people in the street, for example, and think of itself as apart from them. ... if one is a woman one is often surprised by a sudden splitting off of consciousness, say in walking down Whitehall, when from being the natural inheritor of that civilization, she becomes, on the contrary, outside it, alien, critical. Clearly the mind is always altering its focus, and bringing the world into different perspectives. (Woolf 1973: 92–3)

To Woolf, for a woman in the 1920s to put pen to paper was a political act, because it was necessarily a feminist one. Woolf illustrates this in her 1931 essay 'Professions for Women'. Here, she observes that a 'phantom' prevents most women from writing. This figure is that of 'The Angel in the House', a name taken from the Victorian poem by Coventry Patmore. More generally, the concept was used to show that men's and women's lives belonged in separate spheres: the man's world was that of work and business, the woman's that of the family and the home. Woolf illustrates this division in *Mrs Dalloway*, but a critique of the mentality behind the separation of spheres occurs more clearly in her nonfiction.

SYLVIA TOWNSEND WARNER

Townsend Warner was a poet and musician, as well as novelist. Her first widely successful novel, *Lolly Willowes* (1926) is a helpful contrast to the novels of May Sinclair discussed in the last chapter. Lolly is a middle-aged spinster who escapes her brother's dreary Christian household in London to find freedom and a pagan joy in the countryside. Refashioning herself a witch, she enters into discussion with the devil over the shortcomings of conventional society and its attitudes to women. A feminist riposte to Sinclair's novels of repression, it reads as a fantasy on the benefits of nature and rurality for women in contrast to male-dominated urban respectability.

A campaigner, left-wing activist, and sexual radical, Townsend Warner lived in Dorset and Norfolk with her partner, the poet Valentine Ackland. Her seven novels are highly varied in tone and experimentation as well as subject matter, but her parabolic and fantastical light fiction of the 1920s represents a feminist modernism that is arguably only paralleled by the dark gothic of Djuna Barnes.

In Townsend Warner's 1927 novel *Mr Fortune's Maggot*, a very different approach to the restrictions of religion and sexual repression is again taken from that found in May Sinclair's work. In this story of how the Reverend Timothy Fortune makes one 'convert' in his years as a missionary on the South Sea island of Fanua, Warner critiques adventure fiction, missionary zeal and European colonial leadership in a tale of repressed eroticism. To an extent, along with the writings of Woolf and other contemporary works, such as Radclyffe Hall's 1928 lesbian novel *The Well of Loneliness*, *Mr Fortune's Maggot* represents a new perspective on sexuality and gender in fiction of the period.

The story focuses on a middle-aged missionary in the south seas aiming to win over 'the heathen' to Christianity, but who is instead drawn to the homoerotic experience he finds newly available to him. Warner uses this scenario to explore lesbian themes and employs the familiar template of the colonial adventure to explore an alien space in which men bond through shared trials. This is a familiar trope from, for example, H. Rider Haggard's writings on how European and African males have more in common than do the men and women of either continent. In such adventure fiction as Haggard's, there is often a common sense of honour and brotherhood between men that is disrupted by the introduction of women in the same way that a deterioration in relations between Indians and Anglo-Indians under the Raj was attributed to the influx of memsahibs from Britain, particularly after the end of British East India Company rule. In Haggard's novels, women are either domesticated as potential victims in need of protection or denigrated as evil influences who have enslaved or gained unnatural control over men, but in Townsend Warner's fiction the men themselves are feminized and their metaphysical intercourse leads to homoerotic interactions in ways parallel to the homosocial environments of the public school or even the trenches.

In *Mr Fortune's Maggot*, the convert Lueli still retains an idol, and Reverend Fortune eventually loses his own faith as conscience bites and he realizes he has fallen in love with his only, and false, convert. The story's ending sends Fortune away from the island because, as he disingenuously explains to Lueli, 'It is time'. When he frees himself from Lueli's arms to board the same boat that deposited him on the island years before, he hears news of a 'Great War' of which he has been entirely ignorant. In response, Fortune is 'incapable of comment' as 'everything that was real, everything that was significant, had gone down with the island of Fanua, and was lost for ever' (Townsend Warner 1948: 174). The novel does not make its homosexual aspect too apparent for the contemporary reader, but the combination of religious fervour, colonial power, and sexual denial simmers away in the story's subtext, gently mocking Fortune's folly in the tropics while Europe prepares for a devastating war that contrasts bitterly with the Reverend's south sea idyll.

Undervalued until Virago began to reprint some of her works, Townsend Warner is an important writer, whose novels can be considered in terms of modernist approaches to fiction alongside other women writers who have been reappraised in recent decades, including Elizabeth Bowen, Jean Rhys, and Rosamond Lehmann.

W. B. YEATS AND 'SAILING TO BYZANTIUM' (1926)

The end of the nineteenth century had marked the decisive phase of Irish resistance to English rule, issuing from the Celtic Revival and Gaelic resurgence of the 1890s. Douglas Hyde founded the Gaelic League in 1893, positioning anticolonial Ireland as essentially an agricultural community with a rural identity. At the same time, Yeats himself embarked on forging an Irish identity based on Celtic culture, publishing his collection of folk stories, *The Celtic Twilight*, in the same year. In 1896 he met Lady Gregory, who became a patron and invited Yeats to spend his summers at Coole Park.

Over the next 15 years, Yeats attempted to instigate a National literary revival through a new Irish poetry, a National Theatre, and a unifying Celtic mythology. Lady Gregory encouraged his interest in the stage, which led to the founding of the Irish National Theatre Society in 1902 and, most famously, the Abbey Theatre in 1904.

Born in 1865, many years before most of the modernist writers, Yeats was an important literary mentor to younger poets, especially Ezra Pound, who came to London to seek out Yeats and centre his new literary renaissance on the capital. In parallel, the impact of Pound's new poetry stimulated Yeats, alongside other inspirations, not least of which was the 1916 Easter Rising in Dublin, which revived Yeats's interest in Irish nationalism. Yeats's output from 1889 to 1916 is primarily dramatic and lyric love poetry, but it is in the years following the move to Irish Independence in 1922 that Yeats starts to fashion verse that is considered alongside the work of the younger modernists.

After years in London and trips to the West of Ireland, Yeats returned to Dublin in 1920 to work for the Nationalist cause, publishing anticolonial poems such as 'Easter 1916', 'Sixteen Dead Men', and 'The Rose Tree' (of Irish Nationalism). His political influence on his country exceeds that of any modern English-language poet, but in addition to his public side, Yeats also valorized the role of the romantic dreamer or wild, mystical aesthete. He sometimes called the two personas Owen Aherne and Michael Robartes. Robartes reflects Yeats's private self: his occult interests, his sexual desires, and his idealism. By contrast, Owen Aherne is the public mask. Like many modernists, Yeats's two sides express less a split personality than an attempt to negotiate the divide between public and private life that had become enshrined in the course of the nineteenth century. Consequently, many critics position Yeats as mediating or caught between opposites, and his poetry arises in the tension between them. Therefore, a poem such as 'Sailing to Byzantium', discussed below, might best be seen as describing a half-wish, a desire that the poet knows is impossible, but which his imagination seizes hold of.

In 1900, Yeats wrote 'The Symbolism of Poetry', in which he expresses his belief in inspiration, magic, and transcendence. In effect, Yeats believed there to be emotional and intellectual symbols which, though often personal, were always given by an external force. Mysterious and ultimately indefinable, these symbols evoke the shared human mind and memory. According to Yeats it is symbolism that has the power to move people in poetry. He wanted organic rhythms, an attention to form, an end to anecdotal description and jaunty rhythms, and a turn from reason to imagination.

Yeats had also long been interested in mysticism, and he joined or founded several theosophical societies. A quasi-religious system, theosophy claims to be based on an insight into divine nature and spiritual reality. Yeats's interest in the philosophy of history and mysticism culminated in the writing of his long 1925 book called *A Vision*. On their Sussex honeymoon, Yeats had encouraged his wife to experiment with automatic writing, which proved such a success that he set out to encompass the resulting 'messages' in a comprehensive system. This produced *A Vision*, which describes at great length Yeats's mystical theory of history and civilization. In relation to Yeats's poetry, mysticism is primarily important in terms of Yeats's fascination with unconscious symbolism and his conviction that the occult provided a philosophy of poetry that emphasized the associative power of the imagination.

In 1919 Yeats said of his poetry that it rested on an interest in literary form, his philosophical beliefs and his concern with Irish nationality, all of which he links in his poetry with art, with the cycles of history, and with the potential of Ireland after Independence.

'Sailing to Byzantium', contained in the 1928 volume *The Tower*, is philosophically concerned with the quest for something permanent beyond life's transience, but it is an imaginative voyage to a distant time, which Yeats regarded as unique. On Byzantium, he wrote, in *A Vision*:

> in early Byzantium, maybe never before or since in recorded history, religious, aesthetic and practical life were one, that architects and artificers...spoke to the multitude and the few alike. The painter, the mosaic worker, the worker in gold or silver, the illuminator of sacred books, were almost impersonal, almost perhaps without the consciousness of individual design, absorbed in their subject-matter and that the vision of a whole people. (Yeats 1964: 244)

Yeats wanted a similar unity for Ireland, and much of his work can be seen as a groping towards appropriate forms, in a national literature, mythology and theatre. So, in 'Sailing to Byzantium' as the poem distances itself from youth and violence, Yeats is personally concerned with transience and the destruction of things that should be valued. This is how he feels about the civil war in Ireland following independence, although he transfers it onto Byzantium. His own position is one of impotence as the various Irish nationalist factions fight for supremacy and, in the process, destroy their own country and its heritage. His equivalent to Eliot's Tiresias is the golden bird that Yeats envisages should embody his soul so that he may sing of the past, present and future on his golden bough. Taken outside of ordinary time, the poet transcends his aging body and inhabits in Byzantium a pure world of mind and soul.

Here, as elsewhere, the overriding impression is of an individual stuck between different forces, public and private, social and personal. Yeats is best seen as oscillating between and negotiating opposites, with his poetry produced through and expressing the tension between them.

EZRA POUND

While Eliot's and, to a lesser extent, Yeats's poetry offers better known examples of modernist verse, Pound has been repeatedly acknowledged as both the central protagonist of the modern literary movement of the period and also the person most responsible for the new bearings of English poetry from the 1910s onward. Eliot and Pound commented on each other's work extensively and shared both reading lists and numerous attitudes, aesthetic and political. Pound's emphasis, however, is far more on the individual, on psychology, and on the ability of the arts to promote individual liberty – a tendency that inclined Pound against the state or political institutions and towards anarchism and the aristocratic freedoms promoted by the extreme right wing, especially the Italian leader Mussolini.

Pound's principal intervention has been noted earlier as the founding of imagism, but the War was to effect quite a change on his outlook, turning his poetic attention to the relationships between culture, economics and politics. After the war, despite establishing imagism, Pound also found that its very popularity now indicated that the approach had done all it could to push poetry forward and that there was a significant danger that poetry would lose its necessary rigour if free verse came to predominate. Pound's 1920 poem 'Hugh Selwyn Mauberley' is his first major attempt to address the sense of postwar crisis, as Eliot also attempts in *The Waste Land*. Over 18 short sections, 'Hugh Selwyn Mauberley' presents two poets, one named in the title and one modelled on Pound but called simply 'E.P.' The question the poem considers is how poetry should be written in the present, though both poets are interested in the poetic forms of the past. The first part of the poem concerns E.P. and notes the seeming absence of 'the sublime' in modern life. The twentieth century has brought mass consumerism, mass democracy, mass media and mass culture, but lost its sense of transcendence, beauty, and artistic importance. E.P. dies an unregarded poet, still 'out of step', as Pound thought himself to be in modern civilization, but he defends himself as an artist against the animus of the twentieth century, which has produced the Great War and commodity fetishism. Then the poem's second part brings in Hugh Selwyn Mauberley, another anachronistic but very different poet, a diffident aesthete who embraces an austere, hard and regular verse. He is the author of most of the first part and its partial critique of E.P., and could be any new young poet of the kind that Pound sought himself to criticize in fashionable artistic circles. The title character in 'Hugh Selwyn Mauberley' retreats to the Pacific Islands and is arguably Pound's final farewell to his old poetic selves. He would now move from aesthetics to broader social concerns.

In line with this, towards the end of the war Pound also started on his enormous project intended to explain modern civilization, *The Cantos*. As a complete cycle of verses, these would remain unfinished at his death, but their magazine publication began in 1917, and in 1925 the first 16 were published in book form. *The Cantos* combine in poetry a range of different types of writing, such as historical accounts, anecdotes, narratives and extensive citation, with Pound's commentary. They also contain lines and quotations from many languages, including the use of Chinese characters.

The poem cycle has considerable geographical breadth as well as a wide range of references to economics, culture, history and politics. A modern epic, *The Cantos* have 120 sections, but little overall form, a fact that Pound regretted, though in his early plans they were to follow more closely the structure of Hell, Purgatory and Paradise, in a kind of sequel to Dante's *Divine Comedy*. Pound himself called them a ragbag, but those written after the Second World War and known as 'The Pisan Cantos', for example, are considered a broadly coherent whole.

Here, we are most concerned with the first Cantos, published in 1925. Like *The Waste Land*, they concern themselves with the disintegration of modern civilization, which has produced the Great War. There are, for example, the 'hell' Cantos, 14 and 15, which berate bankers and hack writers as well as, in thinly disguised form, the war leaders and arms-traders. Like Eliot and Joyce, Pound employed the 'mythic method', bringing events and people in the present into perspective by making comparisons with those of the past. Pound presents world history in terms of descents (into Hades) and metamorphoses (drawing on Ovid) apparent in cultures and in persons, but these themes sit at quite a high level, and the surface of the text appears to the first-time reader as a kaleidoscope of references, often arcane, which can only be contained by the use of myth as an ordering principle. As means to arrange and present his material, Pound also made use of the Japanese Noh drama (gathering together and layering ideas around one theme) and of the dramatic monologues of Robert Browning (and particularly *Sordello*, using a narrator with several speakers in turn). Thus, at the beginning of *The Cantos* he uses Odysseus as an orchestrator of the dead, who will speak directly to the reader. Subsequent Cantos within this first set from the mid-1920s draw on classical myth, renaissance history, the medieval troubadours, and a discussion of the insidious effect of the profit motive in economic life, before the final descent into the hell Cantos mentioned above.

The Cantos assert the importance of the individual voice, so important throughout Pound's poetry, but also foreground the necessity of mediation, whether it be in the form of translation or cultural transmission. Pound's epic is, for many critics, the most ambitious poem in twentieth-century literature and its scope has suggested to many subsequent poets that the limits of poetry could be expanded to include almost anything. Attempts at paraphrasing *The Cantos* are also a reminder that, while modernism furthered the cause and use of poetic prose, the explication of complex modernist poetry into prose cannot avoid reductive paraphrase as substitute for the polyphonic resonance, and difficulty, of the poem.

THE HARLEM RENAISSANCE AND BEYOND

It has been observed that the first African-American artistic rebirth took place at the turn of the century. In 1901, the black critic and poet William Stanley Braithwaite pronounced that 'We are at the commencement of a "negroid" renaissance ... that will have as much importance in literary history as the much spoken of and much praised Celtic and Canadian renaissance' (quoted in Gates: 164). The reason for this confidence was a growth in prominent African-American artistic expression from such as the poet Paul Laurence Dunbar, the novelists Pauline Hopkins and Charles Chesnutt, and the essayists W. E. B. Du Bois and Anna Julia Cooper. However, it was not for another two decades that the Negro Literary Movement, foretold at the turn of the century, emerged and became centred on a Manhattan neighbourhood.

In Harlem, a new generation of black writers and artists in the 1920s came to greater national attention in the United States. Poets such as Countee Cullen and Langston Hughes, the 'poet of Harlem', achieved prominence alongside Jamaican-born Claude McKay and polymath James Weldon Johnson. Many novelists depicted the life of the 'New Negro' while white culture embraced and appropriated African-American music and style. With roots in the imagist movement, Jean Toomer published his masterpiece, *Cane*, in 1923, but its significance was not recognized for many decades. It is a literary work that brings together fragments, short stories and poetry in one book. Its formal experimentation is partly an attempt to combine the elements of the African-American experience. Toomer was a light-skinned black man and *Cane*, like the work of Nella Larsen, is concerned with the practice and purpose of 'passing' as a way to explore the black experience alongside formal use of the 'call and response' interaction of church sermonizing.

Larsen was one of the leading women writers of the Renaissance who found a home in Harlem, where African-Americans in the 1920s were discovering new social and artistic urban lives. Her novels are distinctive in their portrayal of sexuality and ethnicity in relation to the figure of the new woman among the emerging black bourgeoisie. Larsen's work is modernist in its presentation of both a new identity and identity in crisis; her novels follow searches for an inner self amid feelings of duality and double consciousness in the intensity of urban experience.

But the cultural revolution of the Harlem Renaissance, like European modernism, stretched beyond literature, and included artists such as Aaron Douglas, the jazz musician Duke Ellington, the singers Bessie Smith and Paul Robeson, and the dancer Josephine Baker. The diversity evident in this range of artists is underlined by a common exploration of the possibilities of black representation and agency, from the traditional, southern and folkloric, to the urban, northern and progressive. Harlem throughout the 1920s and 1930s can be seen as a centre and a symbol of a flourishing of black art that accompanied the explosion of urban culture and creativity. A city within a city, it was termed the 'Mecca of the New Negro' by the democratic philosopher and educator Alain Locke, whose positive philosophy motivated a significant proportion of the movement as he encouraged artists, writers and musicians to look to Africa for their roots and their inspiration.

The work of the Harlem Renaissance epitomized a wider realization among blacks and whites that innovative aesthetic techniques and approaches contained the subversive possibilities of a kind of passing in which not only did white artists take black art forms, masks and stances, but also black artists could appropriate white sensibilities, activating a new ethnic agenda on practices of *signifying* (subversive play and parody) alongside a call to newness and reinvention.

Michael North argues:

> Writers as far from Harlem as T. S. Eliot and Gertrude Stein reimagined themselves as black, spoke in a black voice, and used that voice to transform the literature of their time. In fact, three of the accepted landmarks of literary modernism in English depend on racial ventriloquism of this kind: Conrad's *Nigger of the 'Narcissus'*, Stein's 'Melanctha', and Eliot's *The Waste Land*. If the racial status of these works is taken at all seriously, it seems that linguistic mimicry and racial masquerade were not just shallow fads but strategies without which modernism could not have arisen. (North, 1993: Preface)

Like Picasso's use of African masks, the adoption, or appropriation, of a black persona allowed Stein in 'Melanctha' to flout the styles and conventions she wished to escape in order to represent fully both her life and a new twentieth-century form of writing. Stein's use of the mask metaphor for modern cultural experience itself derives from features of African, Latin, Anglo and Jewish traditions in American and Spanish cultures, because of their racially and verbally composite character. Also, while recognizing that there was an 'uneasy convergence' between high modernism and colonialism, Simon Gikandi notes that 'For many Caribbean writers and intellectuals, creolization has come to represent a unique kind of Caribbean modernism, one that resists the colonizing structures through the diversion of the colonial language and still manages to reconcile the values of European literacy with the long-repressed traditions of African orality' (Gikandi 1992: 16). Considering writers from George Lamming and Sam Selvon to Wilson Harris and Paule Marshall, Gikandi argues: 'this modernism, which is closely related to creolization, develops as a narrative strategy and counter-discourse away from outmoded and conventional modes of representation associated with colonial domination and colonizing cultural structures' (Gikandi 1992: 5). While Anglo-American modernism often sought to escape history through aesthetics, Caribbean writers needed to exorcise the enslavement and ahistorical positioning of colonial subjectivity through the use of avant-garde techniques.

F. SCOTT FITZGERALD AND THE JAZZ AGE

'The Jazz Age' was the term coined by Fitzgerald to describe the hedonism of the 'Roaring Twenties'. After the Great War and up to the 1929 Great Depression, commercial music gained enormously in popularity as leisure time increased, prosperity came to the United States, and the stock market soared. Despite the introduction of prohibition in 1920, the pursuit of pleasure seemed to be moving increasingly to the fore in the decade, as leisure activities and indulgence overtook traditional values such as the work ethic. The shift was accompanied by the widespread embrace of technological change, with the great increase in mass use of cars, air travel and the telephone.

An author of novels and short stories, Fitzgerald was a writer who both depicted and critiqued the new lifestyles of affluent America. He completed just four novels in his lifetime, with a fifth about Hollywood, entitled *The Love of the Last Tycoon*, left unfinished. His first novel, *This Side of Paradise*, published in 1920, is a lyrical and autobiographically informed study of contemporary youth corrupted by greed and self-promotion. In terms of experimentation, it is chiefly interesting in its blend of forms: free verse poems, letters, and dramatic narrative fiction. *The Beautiful and Damned* is another morality tale critiquing an aimless generation and drawing on Fitzgerald's own life experiences. Published in 1922, it is a study of socialite aspirations and a troubled marriage among the well-to-do café society on the East Coast.

Fitzgerald's romantic lyricism is generally thought to culminate in his third novel, *The Great Gatsby*, which appeared three years after *The Beautiful and Damned*. Jay Gatsby, the enigmatic figure at the centre of the novel, is an example of a man supposedly living the American Dream, but whose life and fate prove to be nightmarish. The novel's narrative, in some ways conventionally melodramatic, is matched with a first-person narrator who unfolds the story of another man in a way that is reminiscent of Ford's *The Good Soldier* and, especially, Conrad's *Lord Jim*. The allusive imagery and rich language deepen an unconventionally plotted novel that moves across time periods: a Conradian structural technique Fitzgerald would take much further in his next novel. The narrator is the unmarried Midwesterner Nick Carraway, who looks back on his experiences in New York and Long Island in the summer of 1922. The book's central intrigue is the title character, who throws lavish parties at his palatial home and who is the subject of countless rumours. Sounding a familiar theme, Nick learns that his neighbour, Gatsby, was unable to marry Daisy, now married to Tom Buchanan, when he was a poor soldier, and that Gatsby has amassed his wealth principally to prove his worth to her. Epitomizing the preference for easy gains that Fitzgerald lamented in the 1920s, Gatsby has, in fact, made his fortune illegally through bootlegging, gambling, fraud, and so on. He has bought his present house because of the view it affords of Daisy's, and his only interest in throwing parties is to attract Daisy there. Nick is able to reintroduce Gatsby to Daisy, and there is a period in which their romance may be rekindled, but tragedy follows, ending with Gatsby's sacrifice of himself for Daisy and his consequent murder.

The novel is also notable for its highly rich use of symbols. One of the most important of these is a pair of bespectacled eyes on a neglected opticians' advertising hoarding that the characters repeatedly pass in their cars as they drive back and forth to New York. These huge painted eyes look on the decadence and hollowness of the characters' lives and variously suggest a judgemental gaze, a loss of vision in society, or the blank stare of a now dead god. Fitzgerald's prose is compressed and taut, but suffused with a wistful romanticism that suggests a fallen world after the Great War and a whole generation who have lost their way. The novel is highly contemporary in its modern references and its setting, but there is also an unspecified nostalgia and a longing for innocence that gives the book wide appeal as an iconic text of the twentieth-century's twin features of rising prosperity and shocking violence: the birth of mass consumerism and mass destruction.

Conceived soon after *The Great Gatsby*, but many troubled years in gestation, Fitzgerald's final complete novel, *Tender is the Night*, was partly written while his wife Zelda was hospitalized for schizophrenia. Published in 1934, it is the story of a glamorous couple living in the south of France: the psychoanalyst, Dick Diver, whose wife Nicole is also his patient. His practice is built on her money, and their marriage is based on their quest to find a cure for Nicole's neuroses. As the years have progressed, however, Dick's life, mental health, and highly promising career have deteriorated as he uncharacteristically turns to drink and violence as outlets for his frustration. The novel is usually seen as a study of disintegration that also depicts how, as Dick weakens with each new failure, Nicole becomes stronger. Before posthumous publication of the incomplete *The Love of the Last Tycoon*, initially as *The Last Tycoon*, this was Fitzgerald's final study of American identity and the modern condition after the Great War, but for once, resituated in the wasted battleground of Europe.

WILLIAM FAULKNER

Faulkner's first two novels, *Soldiers' Pay* (1927) and *Mosquitoes* (1927), were well-received, while his third, *Sartoris* (1929), introduced the fictional county of Yoknapatawpha that was to be a setting for much of his subsequent fiction, including his already completed masterpiece *The Sound and the Fury*, which was also published in 1929. A commercial failure on release, the book grew in reputation to become probably Faulkner's most admired and studied novel.

The Sound and the Fury is written in four chapters, each with a different narrator: the brothers Benjy, Quentin and Jason, followed by a third-person narrator. Three of the chapters are set on the Easter weekend of the year before publication, and all four are focused on the once-grand Compson family, who have now fallen on hard times. The novel's title is a quotation from the last act of Shakespeare's *Macbeth* that characterizes life as 'a tale / Told by an idiot, full of sound and fury / Signifying nothing'. While the two subsequent narrators from the Compson family could be made to fit this description, it most clearly refers to the first section, which is narrated by the mentally handicapped Benjy Compson. This is a fragmented and non-linear story that flits about between the different concerns Benjy has at any one moment; much of Benjy's broken story cannot be pieced together until after the revelations of subsequent chapters. Given this is Easter weekend, it is also no coincidence that Benjy is 33 years old, as Christ was at his crucifixion. The two people who show concern and care for Benjy are his sister Caddy and a servant, Dilsey, both of whom will have significant roles later in the story. The section is often found difficult to decipher, because Faulkner is rendering the story solely through Benjy's language and preoccupations. In the hope of hearing the word 'caddy', he spends much of his life beside the golf course that the family has had to sell to meet its debts. Benjy has no sense of time, and his thought processes are associative, so the gap between 1928 and the time of the next section does not exist for him.

The second section is set 18 years earlier, on 2 June 1910, and comprises the self-told story of bright but unstable Harvard student

Quentin Compson's suicide. He is a chivalrous idealist deeply concerned with purity, and particularly the virginity of his sister.

Quentin's suicide is linked to the fact that Caddy has become pregnant by a man named Dalton Ames. To share her fate, Quentin claims that the child is the result of incest, but Caddy decides she must marry as soon as possible. She thus both marries and, on discovery that she is carrying an illegitimate child, is banished by Herbert Head in 1910. Devastated by her loss, Quentin walks the streets of Harvard with his narration moving between thoughts of the past and experiences in the present. All the time he is broodingly preoccupied with Caddy, suicide, and the fallen South, such that his monologue is confused and sometimes misleading. By the end of the section, as Quentin nears his death by drowning, the language deteriorates to such a degree that sense, syntax and punctuation almost completely breakdown. Later in the year, Caddy gives birth to a daughter, who is named after her dead brother and known as Miss Quentin.

Section Three returns to the present and takes place on Easter Friday. It is told by the third brother, Jason, who has become the head of household. He makes himself guardian of his hypochondriac mother, Caroline, and his wilful niece, Miss Quentin, but is a cynical materialist whose principal thought is how to increase his wealth. Jason is appalled by the behaviour of his banished sister, Caddy, and by the waywardness of her daughter.

The final section is set on Easter Sunday and employs an omniscient narrator. It focuses on Dilsey, the matriarch among the servants and the principal caregiver to the Compsons. It is she and her children who effectively look after Benjy. On this most holy of days in the Christian calendar, Dilsey attends church and draws great support from her faith, but also compassion for the Compson family, despite her ill-treatment at their hands. Dilsey becomes the witness of the Compson's disintegration, pointed out by Jason's angry pursuit of Miss Quentin, who has run off with his life savings, which includes money Jason has embezzled from her. The end of the story returns to Benjy and the family's need to keep him from wailing as a different course is taken in the horse carriage from the church to the graveyard. His fury ever-present as he seemingly compensates for his lowly position as a menial farm store worker by pursuing power under the guise of responsibility for his family, Jason has to calm Benjy as he has to tame Miss Quentin and console his mother.

The novel is especially notable for its formal experimentation. There is, most clearly, the unusual time scheme and the use of multiple unreliable narrators, but also, for example, extensive employment of stream of consciousness and the frequent use of italics when the narrative moves into the past in flashback. With extensive utilization of the Jamesian principle of showing rather than telling, the novel is rich enough to withstand myriad readings, and its complexity is both technical and psychological. There is a strong ethical drive to the novel in its approach to issues of ethnicity and gender, with Dilsey and Caddy emerging as the two rocks on which the story stands. Faulkner saw the latter as the hero of the novel, though she hardly appears.

In late 1929, Faulkner wrote another experimental and ultimately highly influential novel, *As I Lay Dying* (1930), while working as a night supervisor at the power plant of the University of Mississippi, his alma mater. Like the earlier novel, it focuses on a single family, but this time they are impoverished workers transporting the corpse of Addie Bundren cross-country to Jefferson. Despite numerous setbacks, her husband and children persevere in their endeavour over nine days, as the story is told in chunks of a few pages narrated by one or another of the many characters. Sometimes the narration is presented in demotic dialect, but at other times it reaches the richness of poetry as the deep emotion of the characters transforms the language in which Faulkner presents their plight. The daughter is concealing her pregnancy, one son's mind oscillates between genius and madness, and the deceased woman herself has a passage in which she remembers the love-affair that resulted in one birth. Faulkner's method has been seen as a reflection of his uncertainty of purpose, but for those readers who respond to emotion and the dense psychological portrait of conflicted characters, his works have a deep appeal by bringing the techniques developed by James, Conrad and Joyce to a sustained portrayal of the decline of the American South. Faulkner continued to produce complex works in the 1930s, such as *Light in August* (1932) and *Absalom, Absalom* (1936), that would at least come to be very highly regarded after he won the Nobel prize for literature in 1949.

MODERNIST AMERICAN POETRY

While writing poetry in his spare time, Wallace Stevens spent most of his working life in the legal department of insurance companies, eventually becoming a vice president in the 1930s. Though be began publishing in magazines much earlier, it was not until 1923 that his first volume, *Harmonium*, appeared, when Stevens was in his mid-forties. The volume had a dramatic effect on American poetry containing now well-known pieces such as 'Thirteen Ways of Looking at a Blackbird', 'Ploughing on Sunday', 'Earthy Anecdote', 'The Snow Man', 'Anecdote of the Jar' and 'Sunday Morning'. Sensual, musical, elegant, and often parodic, the poems marry imagism with a romantic spirit and intriguing symbolism. Like the run of romantic poets from Keats to Yeats, Stevens believed in the primacy of the imagination and its ability to reveal or refashion reality. Stevens sought 'the poem of the mind in the act of finding / What will suffice' ('Of Modern Poetry'), and thought that the poet gives to life the imaginative beliefs fundamental to its conception.

Perhaps of most significance in his approach was the fact that Stevens tried to conjoin the poet's imagination and the real world, while conscious of the many dissonances between the aspirations of art and the actuality of day-to-day living. He also argued there was a need for secular beliefs to compensate for the modern loss of religious feeling, for poetry to address the qualities and nature of perception and imagination, and ultimately for poetry to aspire to what he later called the pure romantic vision of 'supreme fictions'. Stevens is not a great experimenter in terms of form, but his meditations on poetry, his use of sense perception, and his deployment of a personal mythology combine in a rich use of vocabulary, symbolism and linguistic originality that have increased his reputation steadily since the Second World War.

One of the poems in *Harmonium* is 'Nuances of a Theme by Williams', in which Stevens adds two verses of commentary onto William Carlos Williams's poem 'El hombre'. Williams was a life-long friend of Pound and Hilda Doolittle who followed a career as a paediatrician while writing, influencing, and shaping avant-garde poetry in New York. Like Yeats's Celtic Revival in Ireland, Williams wished to shape an American poetry that used the rhythms, ideas, and speech patterns of his country. Unlike Robert Frost's use of New England idioms in his poetry, Williams, from his debut collections *Poems* (1909) and *The Tempers* (1913), tried to give voice to the whole migrant and multiracial culture of the United States. It was with *Al Que Quiere!* in 1917 that his departure from Shakespeare and the romantics became apparent, and his short lyrics such as

'The Red Wheelbarrow' came to resemble the hard verbal precision of imagism. As an experimental modernist, Williams published his most intriguing work in the 1920s, in the poetry collections *Kora in Hell* (1920) and *Spring and All* (1923), plus the hybrid historical fiction of *In the American Grain* (1925), a series of character studies that, on the one hand, criticize the Puritans for their lack of positive engagement with the New World and its peoples and, on the other hand, offer praise for those who have. Williams stressed links with the American land (following the native example of Whitman, rather than the transatlantic one of Eliot) and with the concrete materiality of lived experience. His poetry of the 1920s picks up lessons from cubism, Dadaism and surrealism to showcase reflections on art in the world in a fragmented, collage style that incorporated prose within verse.

A third important modernist American poet is Marianne Moore. First published in the *Egoist* and *Poetry* in 1915, her earliest collections appeared in 1921 (*Poems*) and 1924 (*Observations*). Moore also became editor of the *Dial* from the mid-1920s to its cessation in 1929, thus influencing a sizable portion of the modernist canon at the time. Much admired by her contemporaries, Moore's work exemplifies aspects of innovative modernist poetry. Pound thought her writing epitomized a 'dance of the intelligence' in words, and her style and approach drew admiration from Williams and Stevens, who cited for praise her 'powers of observation' and her 'skilful expression'. *Observations* displays the content and form of her work well, wherein she also describes her desire for poets that are 'literalists of the imagination', pictured as composing 'imaginary gardens with real toads in them' ('Poetry'). In this poem, typical of her free verse, her emphasis is on poetry that strives to be 'genuine', which is akin to the truth in art that Pound felt fundamental to the best verse. Moore uses ordinary language, but peppers it with copious quotation marks, arch observation, waspish wit and startling, but revealing, imagery. Alongside this she employs unexpected juxtapositions, as in her 1923 long poem 'Marriage,' which contains classical, Judeo-Christian, and Shakespearean allusions alongside fashion ads and contemporary women's magazines. As a pioneering feminist work of high modernism 'Marriage' deserves a more prominent place in critical studies beside totemic contemporary works such as *The Waste Land.*

MINA LOY AND DJUNA BARNES

Loy and Barnes were two modernist writers deeply aware of the potential in literature for a reexamination of definitions of gender and sexuality. The personal and artistic career of Mina Loy parallels the development of several strains of modernist thinking, ranging from decadence to Dadaism, futurism to feminism. Born in London as Mina Gertrude Lowy, Loy was a radical poet involved with Gertrude Stein and Ezra Pound, modern art and futurism, free verse and free love, who composed poems from 1910 onwards that gained a contemporary notoriety. They address such subjects as 'Joyce's *Ulysses*', 'Brancusi's Golden Bird', 'The Ineffectual Marriage' and 'Parturition'. Published in the 1914 inaugural issue of *Trend*, 'Parturition' is probably the first direct poem written by a woman about giving birth, and its form mimics a woman's contractions in labour. Her characteristic wit and use of violent imagery in poems such as 'Love Songs' led one of Loy's editors to declare: 'To reduce eroticism to the sty was an outrage, and to do so without verbs, sentence structure, punctuation, even more offensive' (Scott: 233).

Considered to be a major innovator of modernist poetics, Loy's poetry arose from the unusual combination of her experience in Europe prior to World War I, her close association with radicals like Marinetti, and her mixture of feminist with metaphysical concerns. Loy adapted to her own pictorial ends the way in which Stein brought spatiality to the foreground in two sequences of linked portrait poems from this period, 'Three Moments in Paris' and 'Italian Pictures'. In 'Aphorisms [on Futurism]', which appeared as the central literary text in the January 1914 issue of *Camera Work*, Loy crossed the prose poem with the manifesto, adapting elements of Marinetti's '*arte di far manifesti*' – the inventive typography, bold layout and attention-grabbing aphorisms. In her poetry written during the First World War, she stressed the cultural limitations imposed on women's potential and she analyzed the psychological effects of acquiescing in femininity. During the 1920s, she embarked on a defence of modernism and a related critique of the symbolists' and the decadents' aesthetic tenets. *Lunar Baedecker*, her 1923 book of poems, gave prominence to her vision of the artist's special calling and social autonomy: she adapted familiar concepts to praise an approach based on the aesthetic practice of the cosmopolitan artistic circles she encountered in Paris. Loy's distinctive method was one of working through a collage-like juxtaposition of abstractions, images and allusions. In poems such as 'Anglo-Mongrels and the Rose' she displays futuristic devices of disparate images, fragmented syntax and minimal punctuation, with white space, capitalization and dashes to indicate emphasis and pause.

On Mina Loy's relationship with modernism, it may be deduced that her marginalization from the canon constructed in the 1950s and 1960s depended on her radical critique of marriage and heterosexuality. Labelled as 'cerebral' Loy's work in fact often focuses on the economic situation of women as well as sexuality and intellectual ability. Loy could not overlook her own difference from the masculinist norm and challenged the futurist vision built on the notion of sameness by undoing repressive aspects of social hierarchy.

Loy's influence on modernism has often been underestimated, as has, more generally, the role of the feminist movement in changing aesthetics. Another important female modernist is Djuna Barnes, who also subverted traditional genres. Her hybrid palimpsest texts, such as *Ryder* and *Ladies Almanack*, change styles from one chapter to another and are characterized by ambiguity and obscurity; but most notable, perhaps, is Barnes's repeated portrayal of violence within the patriarchal family.

Born in 1892 in New York and educated at home by a polygamous father, Barnes lived a complex life in both Paris and London. She is chiefly known for a 'gothic modernism', influenced by nineteenth-century vampire fiction, the Pre-Raphaelites, and early European horror cinema, but also by the mystics Aleister Crowley and Madame Blavatsky. Many of her early poems combine modernist conceptions of gender with a distinctly Gothic vocabulary that details 'trysts' between living lovers and dead 'beloveds'. Drawing on images of mortality and forbidden desire familiar from Tennyson, Rossetti, Poe and Le Fanu, Barnes created pastiche narratives that combine the imagery of modern lesbian relationships with relations between the living and the resurrected dead. It has been conjectured that Barnes's 'aesthetic strategy' possibly comes from her grief at the death of her lover, Mary Pyne. With titles like 'The Flowering Corpse' and 'Hearsed Up in Oak', her imagery certainly draws on legends of death and exhumation, touching on images of the living-dead bride or vampire women, though certain images of the occult in her work draw on events and people in Paris during Barnes's stay there in the 1920s.

Barnes's poetry became more complex throughout her life. While early lyric poems are conventional in form, later, posthumously published works are more difficult and clearly modernist. In her poetry (*The Book of Repulsive Women*, 1915), and short stories (*A Book,* 1923; *A Night among the Horses*, 1929) and in the challenging feminist explorations of *Ryder* (1928), *Ladies Almanack* (1928) and *Nightwood* (1936), 'Barnes examined not only the failures of representational reality but also – as shown in the selections here included – the asymmetries of age and power and the contradictions inherent in gender definitions that undercut family intimacies, encoding complex modes of eroticism for which we as yet have no literary typology' (Broe: 20–1).

ASPECTS OF THE NOVEL (1927) AND
A SURVEY OF MODERNIST POETRY (1927)

While this study has generally looked at the drama, fiction and poetry of the principal modernist decades, Woolf's *A Room of One's Own* was an important exception, and two other books by practitioners of fiction and poetry are particularly notable works of literary criticism from the period. E. M. Forster's *Aspects of the Novel* began as a series of Clark Lectures given at Trinity College, Cambridge. An idiosyncratic survey of fiction from Defoe to Joyce, these talks were written at a time when Forster had finished with novel writing. The lectures were delivered between January and March 1927 and were less academic expositions than one author's perspective on literary history, style and form. One influential attendee, the critic F. R. Leavis, thought them 'intellectually null', but they were still a great success. On the strength of the lectures, King's College offered Forster a three-year fellowship, which he accepted.

In the lectures, Forster defines the novel as any work of prose fiction, which he goes on to discuss in terms of character, plot, fantasy, symbolism, pattern and rhythm. The most important of these, to a discussion of his own fiction, is arguably the last, because Forster and his critics have used the term 'rhythm' to refer to the structural use of leitmotifs or 'repetitions with variation' in fiction that depends upon expanding symbols. 'Rhythm' then refers to the repeated use of phrases, words, incidents, or characters to create a rhythmic effect in the evolution of a text's themes. The technique is apparent in Forster's *A Passage to India*, and in particular in the use made of the echo that haunts Adela and Mrs Moore after their visit to the Marabar Caves, but it can also be applied to readings of Joyce or Proust, whose utilization of symbolism and repeated images is clear in *Dubliners* and *A la recherché du temps perdu*, respectively.

In the most well-known section of the lectures, Forster describes his view of character, from which all other aspects of the novel follow. Most noteworthy is the distinction between round and flat characters, the former two-dimensional and the latter as real to readers as their own acquaintances. Forster felt that all art aspires to the condition of music, in terms of intellectual depth and emotional effect, such that the best model for the novel was, in fact, the symphony.

Also published in 1927, Robert Graves and Laura Riding's *A Survey of Modernist Poetry* contains one of the very earliest employments of the term 'modernist' to describe recent experiments in poetry. It discusses a considerable number of the greater and lesser British and American poets still recognized today as modernist, including e. e. Cummings, Ezra Pound, Wallace Stevens, T. S. Eliot, Edith Sitwell and Marianne Moore, with particular emphasis given to Gertrude Stein in a long conclusion. The book is, in part, a defence of the claim that poetry must be difficult and demanding for the reader, a contention most famously made by T. S. Eliot. Graves and Riding maintain that this is partly an argument over clearness, taking the view that clarity of expression often requires complexity. They also reiterate the view that poetry is concerned with feeling, explaining that modernist poetry attempts to 'break down antiquated literary definitions of people's feelings' and to 'discover what it is we are really feeling'. Most importantly, Graves and Riding put forward the view that poetry is to be defined and redefined by poets, not delineated by accepted traditional notions of what it should be. Their contention is that, despite experiments in typography and nonlinguistic reference points, the poem 'is not the paper, not the type, not the spoken syllables. It is as invisible and as inaudible as thought'. Poetry is language, feeling and new thought activity.

The contemporary state of poetry in the 1920s reflected a need to contest its terms, but Riding and Graves both criticize many of the current avant-garde writers, including H. D. and William Carlos Williams, and imagine a different future, in which 'it is not impossible that there will be resumption of less eccentric, less strained, more critically unconscious poetry'.Riding and Graves's survey went on to influence the method and practice of New Criticism, largely through the work of William Empson. Most significantly, it was their close attention to a thorough analysis of the words on the page that affected future directions in reading literature, and modernist poetry in particular.

PRACTICAL CRITICISM

While schools still taught Englishness through literature, after the war universities were forging a new method of literary study centred upon 'analysis'. Following the founding of the first modern English degree at Cambridge in 1917, it was in the 1920s that English literature started to cease its role as one element in the study of 'national character' and established itself as an academic discipline devoted to poring over its own texts alongside and in the manner of Biblical studies.

English literature thrived in universities after the Great War, before which it had been seen as a very poor imitation of classics and chiefly useful in its relation to language or history. Over the 1920s, the subject of English literary studies was transformed from an amateurish subject for dilettantes to a highly professional field of enquiry, from an upstart in the academy to one of the central disciplines in the humanities. This metamorphosis was achieved by a close attention to the moral and social values expressed by the language of individual texts, a detailed reading of the specific words used by the writer on every line. Through such rigorous scrutiny, the traditions, sensibilities, emotions and spirituality of life since Chaucer could be reconstructed to provide a map of national writing and culture.

The literary canon, which is still largely intact today, was assembled in this decade as the criteria of judgment changed from the largely undiscriminating principle of good writing (such as a direct 'masculine' style) to questions of complexity, seriousness, richness, sensitivity and organic form. Fine literature no longer promoted simple patriotic feeling, but uplifted the readers and placed them in the vanguard of civilized manners and morality, a view which persisted until the horrors of Auschwitz revealed to European minds what had been apparent in the colonies for centuries: the compatibility of high culture with brutality.

The most influential group of critics surfaced at Cambridge. These radicals, F. R. and Q. D. Leavis, I. A. Richards and others, were not sons and daughters of the aristocracy like the prewar professors, but the children of tradespeople from the provinces. The critical approach taken by this coterie of thinkers was 'practical criticism', which was to evolve into 'New Criticism', a practice of close reading that promoted the minute analysis of a text (for ambiguity, irony, paradox, and so forth) in isolation from any historical context. The literary work or art became divorced from authorial intention, from the reader's private reaction to it, and from social or political events. Instead, the poem stood as an artefact in itself, an enclosed, meaningful, concrete linguistic object to be analysed by the disinterested critic.

For I. A. Richards, whose *Principles of Literary Criticism* (1924) is a seminal work in the development of English studies, the reading of poetry in the twenties served a quasi-spiritual purpose. In his 1926 book *Science and Poetry*, Richards argued that with the decline of religion and the ascendancy of science, poetry needed to be studied as the greatest example of imaginative achievement. Richards, in certain respects, had the same view of the modern world as Eliot, arguing in 'Poetry and Belief' that there is: 'a sense of desolation, of uncertainty, of futility' such that 'the only impulses which seem strong enough to continue unflagging are commonly so crude that, to more finely developed individuals, they hardly seem worth having. Such people cannot live by warmth, food, fighting, drink and sex alone'. What the world needed was the emotional, spiritual, moral and intellectual sustenance of poetry. Also, at a time when much of the world was disunited, divided and war-weary, Richards's *Practical Criticism* (1929) argued that the purpose of literature was to achieve unity, in terms of meaning, the association of thought and feeling, and the relation between form and content. This perspective, largely applied to the texts of literary history, was in stark contrast to other, mainly European and Marxist, approaches to contemporary modernist literature promoted by the Frankfurt School of critical theorists.

CONCLUSION: LATE MODERNISM

The most famous modernist slogan in English is probably 'make it new', which Ezra Pound employed as a book title in 1934. Though the phrase was used at the tail end of the modernist period, it has often been seen as the rallying cry of twentieth-century experimental literature. But the question arises as to what the writers were making new. A general belief is that modernist literature primarily made form new, particularly through a self-conscious, stylized and poetical approach to all writing.

In poetry, modernism is allied with moves to break away from the iambic pentameter as the basic unit of verse – the first heave, as Ezra Pound put it – to bring in *vers libre*, the principles of imagism and the stances taken in other manifestos. In prose, modernism is associated with the reappraisal of the purposes of linguistic representation. Novelists tried anew to represent consciousness, emotion, perception and meaning through interior monologue, stream of consciousness, tunnelling, defamiliarization, rhythm, irresolution, and so on. Modernist writers therefore strove to modify, if not overturn, existing modes of representation, partly by edging them further towards the complex, abstract or introspective.

Modernism also sought to signal a change in human subjectivity: to make new identities and make anew the idea of the self. The modernist subject is generally seen to be alienated and fragmented, but lamenting the loss of a self that was once coherent and self-sufficient, just as secularists followed Nietzsche in both pronouncing the death of God and grieving over it. This is the view of the modernist self as dualistic or divided, but lamenting the loss of an older, integrated ego.

Here we recall Eliot's Prufrock, Conrad's secret sharers, or Woolf's Mrs Dalloway before the mirror composing her fragments of self into a whole for her party. On the one hand, familiar modernist figures are the double, the doppelganger and the alter ego. On the other hand, the self is plural and fragmented, the mind doubled and divided. Consequently, in much modernist writing, thought is dialogic and not monologic, in line with Plato's idea that thinking is a conversation the mind has with itself. In many modernist works, from Joyce's *Ulysses* to Ford's *The Good Soldier*, it requires only one voice to conduct a conversation or even an argument. In the novels of such writers as Dorothy Richardson and May Sinclair (and, later, Lewis Grassic Gibbon) this effect is also apparent in extensive use of the second person, intimating a protagonist who is at once self and other.

Modernism is often summarized by its manifestoes, which is a worthwhile shorthand, given that the manifesto genre itself says something important about modernism. In 1929, 'The Revolution of the Word' manifesto, which was published in the magazine *transition* (signatories to which were also apologists for the sections of Joyce's *Finnegans Wake* published in the same magazine as 'Work in Progress'), refused any obligation for art to communicate. The final four declarations are as follows:

9. WE ARE NOT CONCERNED WITH THE PROPAGATION OF SOCIOLOGICAL IDEAS, EXCEPT TO EMANCIPATE THE CREATIVE ELEMENTS FROM THE PRESENT IDEOLOGY.

10. TIME IS A TYRANNY TO BE ABOLISHED.

11. THE WRITER EXPRESSES. HE DOES NOT COMMUNICATE.

12. THE PLAIN READER BE DAMNED. (in Rainey: 1011)

These are signal themes in modernist aesthetics. André Breton's more famous manifestos also place surrealism 'as far as possible from the desire to make sense' (Breton: 162), but what characterizes the modernist manifestos in general is their refusal of obligations and traditions linked to an ostensibly prior generation.

Whether as creative destruction or education, modernist style is a question of distinctiveness:

The great modernisms were ... predicated on the invention of a personal, private style, as unmistakable as your fingerprint, as incomparable as your own body. But this means that the modernist aesthetic is in some way organically linked to the conception of a unique self and private identity, a unique personality and individuality. (Jameson 1983: 114)

Other critics have argued that modernism had two principal motives: the desire to establish artistic thresholds and the drive to exploit new subject matter thrown up by the speed of 'economic, political, and social change' (Trotter: 290). The forces behind both the desire and the drive were not generated predominantly, let alone exclusively, within Europe, however; for example, Ashcroft, Griffiths and Tiffin representatively argue that many of the various forms of literary experimentation at the turn of the century were products of 'the discovery of cultures whose aesthetic practices and cultural models were radically disruptive of the prevailing European assumptions' (Ashcroft, Griffiths and Tiffin: 156). The confrontation with African art, Indian philosophy, and the alternative aesthetic principles of non-Western countries led to a rejuvenation of European culture, but also infused the crisis represented by modernism in European colonialism, as social, national and religious certainties, weakened by new movements predicated upon gender and class, were also being undermined by exposure to a colonial otherness.

All of these factors went on to inform late modernist works in the 1930s and beyond, when the mainstream of avant-garde experimentation had started to see other movements come to the fore: antimodernism and neorealism in the 1930s, postmodernism and neomodernism after the Second World War. However, the foremost reason for a change in literary dominant around 1930 is arguably social. Most literature began to take its cues from a society and culture concerned with rising unemployment, the aftermath of the Wall Street crash, the rise of fascism, and so on. Another reason is simply generational and modernists such as Pound and Joyce continued to produce experimental writing with large, often mythopoeic structures in a literary style that reflected the preoccupations of an earlier decade. Meanwhile, the noted voices of the literary thirties predominantly reflect a young constituency. In 1930 George Orwell was 27, Graham Greene was 26, Evelyn Waugh 27 and W. H. Auden 23. Samuel Hynes has thus defined the 1930s as a decade focused on writers born in the first 14 years of the century, up to the Great War (Hynes: 1979).

Orwell sums up the change well in his essay 'Inside the Whale':

Quite suddenly, in the years 1930–35, something happens, the literary climate changes. A new group of writers, Auden and Spender and the rest of them, has made its appearance, and although technically these writers owe something to their predecessors, their tendency is entirely different. Suddenly we have got out of the twilight of the Gods into a sort of boy scout atmosphere of bare knees and community singing. The typical literary man ceases to be a cultured expatriate with a leaning towards the church and becomes instead an eager-minded schoolboy with a leaning towards communism. If the keynote of the writers of the twenties is 'tragic sense of life', the keynote of the new writers is 'serious purpose' (Orwell: 177)

The writing of these authors has sometimes been characterized as antimodernist, decidedly realist, with a preference for the importance of subject matter and little concentration on innovation, defamiliarization, alienation, formalism, or individual consciousness. Nevertheless, many writers of the 1930s who are astute social commentators displayed influences of the techniques of modernism, and works like Isherwood's *Goodbye to Berlin* (1939) and Steinbeck's *The Grapes of Wrath* (1939) show a strong indebtedness.

Other young writers, however, followed firmly in the footsteps of the modernists. John Dos Passos in the United States had begun to introduce stream of consciousness techniques into his work, from *Manhattan Transfer* (1925) onwards, but his major impact came with the U.S. trilogy comprising *The 42nd Parallel* (1930), *Nineteen Nineteen* (1932), and *The Big Money* (1936), in which he incorporated newspaper clippings, autobiography, biography and a documentary realism that took modernism in a new direction. Samuel Beckett worked as Joyce's amanuensis and honed his own style of late modernist prose that effected a minimalism and often compassionate antihumanism that anticipated much of postmodernism. Novels such as *Murphy* (1938) and *Watt* (1953, composed 1945) are experimental philosophical works that eschew the mythic mode, but build on the playful linguistic and philosophical excesses of Joyce. In a similar vein are the ludic seriocomic works of Flann O'Brien, such as *The Third Policeman* (1968, composed 1939–40) and *At Swim-Two-Birds* (1939). Another prominent novelist is Malcolm Lowry, chiefly famous for his phantasmagoric Mexican novel *Under the Volcano* (1947), a highly complex late-modernist tour de force which follows the day-in-the-life approach of Joyce's *Ulysses* and Woolf's *Mrs Dalloway*, but which draws on Lowry's personal interests in romanticism, expressionism, symbolism and the cabbala. Set on the Day of the Dead, 2 November 1938, the novel charts the final 12 hours in the life of a British ex-consul in the Mexican town of Quauhnahuac (a fictionalized Cuernavaca). In conventional terms, little happens as 'the Consul' embarks on a drinking spree, while his wife, who has temporarily returned to him, and his brother, who has been fighting in the Spanish Civil War, try to keep him from harm, whether self-inflicted or at the hands of the corrupt Mexican police. The book's fascination lies in its exemplary use of modernist devices: symbolism, expressionist imagery, interior monologue, mythological allusion, time-shifting, fast-cutting, and intensely resonant, rhythmical, poetic prose. Like Joyce's *Ulysses* it is a book about everything: politics, history, Western literature, religion, psychology and human relationships.

Another notable modernist was the Russian-American Vladimir Nabokov, whose works, such as the complex, multilayered *Pale Fire* (1962), a long poem followed by a lengthy commentary by a friend of the supposed author, are intricate experiments with language, form and imagination that find corollaries in the work of English writer B. S. Johnson and the Argentinean Jorge Luis Borges. Such writers play games in labyrinths of their own creation and sit on a borderline between modernism and postmodernism. Other American writers, from Zora Neale Hurston to Ernest Hemingway, Henry Miller to Henry Roth, Ralph Ellison to Richard Wright, wrote novels that were indebted to numerous traditions of writing, including modernist experimentation, while in England authors such as Aldous Huxley and, later, Lawrence Durrell produced highly innovative and experimental fiction.

In American poetry, the modernist baton was taken up by the objectivist poets led by Charles Reznikoff and Louis Zukofsky, who began his lifelong masterwork 'A' in 1927. However, by the 1950s a late modernism was starting to flourish in American poetry and became especially prominent with the work of the L=A=N=G=U=A=G=E poets, the Beats, and the Black Mountain poets fronted by Charles Olson. In British poetry, Hugh MacDiarmid, from *A Drunk Man Looks at the Thistle* (1926) onwards, was the one highly regarded

Scottish modernist poet, mostly using the Lowland Scots of Burns, while the English poet David Jones produced perhaps the finest trench war poem with the epic *In Parenthesis* in 1937, mentioned in Chapter Two in the section on War Poetry. At one time allied with the American objectivist poets, Basil Bunting ploughed a largely solitary furrow in later years and published a modernist free verse epic with *Briggflatts: An Autobiography* in the mid-1960s.

There are other examples of Anglo-American writers promulgating the legacy of modernism, but there are also Anglophone modernisms apparent in other countries. Some of these derive from turn-of-the-century movements, such as the 1900s Bengal art movement; the Jamaican Claude McKay's 1910s articulations, both in Caribbean patois and standard English; the 1920s poetry of the Australian Ken Slessor; or the modernist Hindi poetry of Ajneya and Gajanan Madhav Muktibodh in the 1940s and 1950s (Boehmer: 175). The works of writers such as Wilson Harris, from Guyana, and Gabriel Okara, from Nigeria, also have a great deal in common with modernist forms and styles, though these authors use them to different ends in non-European contexts, while Latin American and Hispanic Caribbean writing has been said to use the poetics of modernism for anticolonial struggle. And in *The Black Jacobins* (1938), the influential critic C. L. R. James made this claim long ago for Aimé Césaire, who uses Eliot's vision of a unified human time in 'The Dry Salvages' to found Negritude. Charles Pollard thus goes on to talk about the 'New World Modernisms' of the Caribbean in writers such as Wilson Harris and Kamau Brathwaite.

Caribbean writers, such as Harris and Césaire, have adopted modernist linguistic strategies and formal approaches, and such realignment of experimental aesthetics has altered modernism's relationship to history, colonialism and political systems through the foundational works of Caribbean modernism: Aimé Césaire's *Cahier d'un Retour Au Pays Natal*, Frantz Fanon's *Black Skin, White Masks*, C. L. R. James's *The Black Jacobins*, George Lamming's *In the Castle of My Skin* and V. S. Naipaul's *A House for Mr Biswas*. A generation of writers, from George Lamming (1927–) to Sam Selvon (1923–94) and Paule Marshall (1929–), has shown that writers of Caribbean origin and influence, far from wishing to escape history like the Anglo-American modernists, sought to exorcise a history of enslavement and the ahistorical positioning of colonial subjectivity.

Edward Said has pointed out that the highpoint of modernism marks the beginning of the end for the European grand narratives that reinforced patriarchy and empire, signalled by the disquieting appearance in Europe of various people from the empire, who by their very presence challenged and resisted familiar metropolitan understandings, aesthetic beliefs and histories in the works of writers such as Eliot, Conrad, Mann, Proust, Woolf, Pound, Lawrence and Joyce. As Henry Louis Gates has observed, it can thus be argued that modernism, as an international web of innovative aesthetic and text-ual practices, was a 'mulatto movement' in which newness came to art through syncretism and fusion, typified by the culture of the Harlem Renaissance. It is almost certainly incontrovertible that the apogee of modernism marks a time at which Western art forms were shaped by international networks. In addition to the influence of Japanese and Chinese art on key figures such as Pound, there is the impact of African art on European artists such as Derain and Picasso, and the popularity of jazz rhythms with classical musicians and also poets. There are the allusions to Indian subjects and imagery in the poetry of Yeats, Eliot's use of African-American references, and Conrad's questioning of the prevailing assumptions of racial super-iority justifying European imperialism. Which is to say that, increas-ingly, even the mainstream canon of modernist writing seems to critics as in some ways a consequence of the growing awareness of different cultures, as anthropology as well as travel and trade brought the trad-itions of other peoples into contemporary Western thinking.

In conclusion, late modernism, like the resurgence of realism that eclipsed it, has been seen as a reaction to the rise of fascism, the creeping shadow of the Second World War, the Great Depression, the rise of mass media and a fading imperialism. The imperial con-traction has allowed a way of reading English literature between modernism and postmodernism as the late modernism of a 'shrink-ing island' (Esty: 2). For Tyrus Miller, who studies the later work of Wyndham Lewis, Mina Loy and Djuna Barnes alongside the new work of Beckett, there is here a central paradox of decadent and forward-looking elements: 'late modernist writing appears a dis-tinctly self-conscious manifestation of the aging and decline of modernism, in both its institutional and ideological dimensions. More, surprising, however, such writing also strongly anticipates future developments, so that without forcing, it might easily fit into a narrative of emergent postmodernism' (Miller: 7). For Fredric

Jameson, such writers persisted with forms of experimentation that were 'unseasonable' because of reasons of isolation or exile (Jameson 1992: 305), and this certainly applies to Beckett, Nabokov, Lowry, Zukofsky, Pound, Lewis, Loy and others. In some ways, then, late modernism is positioned as anachronistic, as a formal and philosophical reaction to changing social forces, and as such, it is noted that the works themselves often deal with decline, death and dead ends. But there is also a reading that sees the legacy of modernism as both a bridge between modernism and postmodernism, and as the catalyst for linguistic and cultural revolutions outside of white American and European preserves.

REFERENCES

Ashcroft, Bill, Gareth Griffiths, and Helen Tiffin. (1989) *The Empire Writes Back*. London: Routledge.

Belsey, Catherine. (1980) *Critical Practice*. London: Methuen.

Boehmer, Elleke. (2002) *Empire, the National, and the Postcolonial, 1890– 1920: Resistance in Interaction*. Oxford: Oxford University Press.

Breton, André. (1972) *The Manifestoes of Surrealism*. Translated by R. Seaver and H. R. Lane. Ann Arbor: University of Michigan Press.

Broe, Mary Lynn. (1990) 'Djuna Barnes', in Bonnie Kime Scott (ed.), *The Gender of Modernism*. Bloomington: Indiana University Press.

Conrad, Joseph. (1944) *Tales of Hearsay and Last Essays*. Harmondsworth: Penguin.

—. (1963a) *The Nigger of the 'Narcissus'*. Harmondsworth: Penguin.

—. (1963b) *Nostromo*. Harmondsworth: Penguin.

—. (1963c) *The Secret Agent*. Harmondsworth: Penguin.

—. (1973) *Heart of Darkness*. Harmondsworth: Penguin.

—. (1992) *An Outcast of the Islands*. Oxford: Oxford University Press.

—. (1994) *Victory*. London: Dent.

—. (1995) *Almayer's Folly*. London: Everyman.

—. (1996) *Lord Jim*. New York: Norton.

—. (2002) *Notes on Life and Letters*. Ed. J. H. Stape. Cambridge: Cambridge University Press.

Doyle, Arthur Conan. (1909) *The Crime of the Congo*. London: Hutchinson.

Eliot, T. S. (1923) '*Ulysses*, Order and Myth', *The Dial*. November.

—. (1932) *Selected Essays*. London: Faber.

—. (1972) 'Tradition and the Individual Talent' (1919), in David Lodge (ed.), *20th Century Literary Criticism*. Essex: Longman.

—. (1975) *Selected Prose of T. S. Eliot*. Ed. Frank Kermode. Faber: London.

Ellmann, Richard and Charles Feidelson (eds.) (1965) *The Modern Tradition*. Oxford: Oxford University Press.

Esty, Jed. (2004) *A Shrinking Island: Modernism and National Culture in England*. Princeton: Princeton University Press.

Faulkner, Peter (ed.) (1986) *A Modernist Reader: Modernism in England 1910–1930*. London: Batsford.

Forster, E. M. (1965) 'The Challenge of Our Time', in *Two Cheers for Democracy*. Harmondsworth: Penguin.

—. (1975) *Howards End*. Harmondsworth: Penguin.

Gates, Henry Louis, Jr. (1997) 'Harlem on our Minds', in Richard J. Powell and David A. Bailey (eds.), *Rhapsodies in Black: Art of the Harlem Renaissance*. London: Hayward Gallery.

Gikandi, S. (1992) *Writing in Limbo: Modernism and Caribbean Literature.* New York: Cornell University Press.

Gurko, Leo. (1979) *Joseph Conrad: Giant in Exile.* London: Macmillan.

Hynes, Samuel. (1972) *Edwardian Occasions.* London: Routledge & Kegan Paul.

—. (1979) *The Auden Generation.* London: Faber.

James, Henry. (1965) 'The Art of Fiction' (1884), reprinted in *Henry James, Selected Literary Criticism.* Ed. M. Shapira. New York: McGraw-Hill, 49–67.

—. (2005) *The Wings of the Dove.* Barnes & Noble: New York.

Jameson, Fredric. (1983) *The Political Unconscious.* London: Methuen.

—. (1992) *Postmodernism: Or, the Cultural Logic of Late Capitalism.* London: Verso.

Joyce, James. (1944) *Stephen Hero.* London: Jonathan Cape.

—. (1960) *A Portrait of the Artist as a Young Man* (1916). Harmondsworth: Penguin.

—. (1969) *Ulysses* (1922). Harmondsworth: Penguin.

—. (1977) *Dubliners* (1914). Hertfordshire: Panther.

Larsen, Nella. (1989) *Quicksand and Passing.* London: Serpent's Tail.

Lawrence, D. H. (1956) *Sons and Lovers.* London: Heinemann.

—. (1960) *Mornings in Mexico and Etruscan Places.* Harmondsworth: Penguin.

—. (1971) *A Selection from Phoenix.* Harmondsworth: Peregrine.

—.(1974) *Apocalypse.* London: Macmillan.

—. (1986) *Women in Love* (1920). Harmondsworth: Penguin.

—. (1993) *The Rainbow* (1915). London: Dent.

Mansfield, Katherine. (1981) *The Collected Stories of Katherine Mansfield.* Harmondsworth: Penguin.

Millard, Kenneth. (1991) *Edwardian Poetry.* Oxford: Clarendon Press.

North, M. (1993) *The Dialect of Modernism.* Oxford: Oxford University Press.

Pollard, Charles W. (2004) *New World Modernisms: T. S. Eliot, Derek Walcott, and Kamau Brathwaite.* Charlottesville, VA: University of Virginia Press.

Orwell, George. (1998) *My Country Right or Left.* London: Folio.

Rainey, Lawrence (ed.) (2005) *Modernism: An Anthology.* Oxford: Blackwell.

Richardson, Dorothy. (1992) *Pilgrimage.* Volume 1. London: Virago.

Roberts, Andrew, and Betty Falkenberg. (2005) *Charlotte Mew Chronology with Mental, Historical and Geographical Connections Linking with Her Own Words.* Middlesex University resource available at http://studymore.org.uk/ymew.htm.

Said, Edward. (1993) *Culture and Imperialism.* London: Chatto & Windus.

Scott, Bonnie Kime (ed.) (1990) *The Gender of Modernism.* Bloomington: Indiana University Press.

Showalter, Elaine (ed.) (1993) *Daughters of Decadence: Women Writers of the Fin-de-Siècle*. London: Virago.

Sinclair, May. (1949) *Mary Olivier: A Life*. London: John Lehmann.

—. (1980) *The Life and Death of Harriett Frean*. London: Virago.

Smith, Stan. (1983) *20th Century Poetry*. London: Macmillan.

Stein, Gertrude. (2008) *Three Lives*. Rockport: Serenity.

Trotter, David. (1993) *The English Novel in History, 1895–1920*. London: Routledge.

Warner, S. T. (1948) *Mr. Fortune's Maggot*. Harmondsworth: Penguin.

Watts, Cedric. (1982) *A Preface to Conrad*. Essex: Longman.

Williams, Raymond. (1989) 'When was Modernism?', in *The Politics of Modernism: Against the New Conformists*. London: Verso, 31–5.

Woolf, Virginia. (1919) 'Modern Fiction' reprinted as 'The Novel of Consciousness', in Ellmann and Feidelson (eds.), 121–6.

—. (1973) *A Room Of One's Own* (1929). London: Grafton.

—. (1976) *Mrs. Dalloway* (1925). London: Grafton.

—. (1986) 'Mr. Bennett and Mrs. Brown' [1924] reprinted, in Peter Faulkner (ed.) *A Modernist Reader: Modernism in England 1910–1930*. London: Batsford.

—. (1988) 'Professions for Women', in *Women and Writing* (1931). London: Women's Press.

—. (2000) *To the Lighthouse*. Oxford: Oxford University Press.

—. (2003) *Orlando*. London: Wordsworth.

Wright, Anne. (1984) *The Literature of Crisis, 1910–22*. London: Macmillan.

Yeats, W. B. (ed.) (1936) *The Oxford Book of Modern Verse*. Oxford: Oxford University Press.

—. (1964) *A Vision*. excerpted in *Yeats: Selected Prose*. Ed. A. Norman Jeffares, London: Macmillan.

—. (1980) *Collected Poems*. London: Macmillan.

INDEX